Welfare Reform in California

Results of the 1999 All-County Implementation Survey

Patricia A. Ebener

Jacob Alex Klerman

RAND **Statewide CalWORKs Evaluation**

Prepared for the California Department of Social Services

LABOR AND POPULATION

The research described in this report was prepared for the California Department of Social Services under Contract No. H38030.

ISBN: 0-8330-2883-9

Published 2001 by RAND
1700 Main Street, P.O. Box 2138, Santa Monica, CA 90407-2138
1200 South Hayes Street, Arlington, VA 22202-5050
RAND URL: http://www.rand.org/
To order RAND documents or to obtain additional information, contact Distribution Services: Telephone: (310) 451-7002; Fax: (310) 451-6915; Internet: order@rand.org

Preface

In response to national welfare reform legislation—the Personal Responsibility and Work Opportunity Reconciliation Act (PRWORA), which was signed in August 1996—California passed legislation on August 11, 1997 that replaced the existing Aid to Families with Dependent Children (AFDC) and Greater Avenues for Independence (GAIN) programs with the California Work Opportunity and Responsibility to Kids (CalWORKs) program. Following an open and competitive bidding process, the California Department of Social Services (CDSS), which administers CalWORKs, awarded a contract to RAND to conduct a statewide evaluation of the CalWORKs program.

This RAND report presents the results of the second of three annual All-County Implementation Surveys (ACIS) to be conducted as part of the statewide evaluation of CalWORKs.

Complete survey responses from the 58 counties are available on the evaluation's web page at http://www.rand.org/CalWORKs. Another report—MR-1777-CDSS, *Welfare Reform in California: State and County Implementation of CalWORKs in the Second Year*, and its Executive Summary, MR-1777/1—combines information from this survey with information from key informant interviews and other sources to present a richer picture of the ongoing implementation of CalWORKs programs in state government and in the focus and follow-up counties participating in the evaluation. Finally, MR-1052-CDSS *(Welfare Reform in California: Results of the 1998 All-County Implementation Survey)* presents the results from the 1998 All-County Implementation Survey. In addition to this process study, there is a parallel impact and cost-benefit study. Preliminary results from that study will be released in October 2000, with the final results in October 2001.

For more information about the evaluation, see http://www.rand.org/CalWORKs or contact:

Jacob Alex Klerman
RAND
1700 Main Street
P.O. Box 2138
Santa Monica, CA 90407-2138
(310) 393-0411 x6289
klerman@rand.org

Aris St. James
CDSS
744 P Street, MS 12-56
Sacramento, CA 95814

(916) 657-1959
astjames@dss.ca.gov

Contents

vi

Figures

Tables

Summary

This report provides the results of the 1999 All-County Implementation Survey (ACIS) conducted as part of RAND's statewide evaluation of CalWORKs. It summarizes the responses of all 58 California counties to questions about their experiences to date with implementing CalWORKs.

The contract between CDSS and RAND for the Statewide CalWORKs Evaluation requires an All-County Implementation Survey (ACIS) in the Fall of 1998, 1999, and 2000 and specifies a response rate of at least 80 percent. This second ACIS was developed in collaboration with CDSS and other state and county agencies and stakeholders. It was reviewed at the county welfare department (CWD) level by the six coordinators in the evaluation's focus counties. The 1999 questionnaire includes 22 questions, many of which were also included in the 1998 questionnaire. The final survey was mailed out September 29, 1999. By November 16, 1999, responses had been received from all 58 California counties.

Overall, the responses to the 1999 ACIS indicate that California counties continue to explore a variety of approaches to CalWORKs program implementation. Their experiences continue to vary significantly throughout the state in terms of what works well and what remains a problem. There are few areas in which all counties agree on a single approach or innovative strategies, though almost all reported some successful strategies. The implementation challenges most frequently noted were use of post employment/job retention services, improving computer systems, and obtaining compliance with required CalWORKs activities. Coordinating the three stages of child care and monitoring and reporting on program performance were the most often cited implementation problems. Fifty-one counties reported that public transportation hinders CalWORKs implementation, and 45 of 58 agree that interagency relationships facilitate implementation. Most counties have seen some CalWORKs caseload decline, and most have added staff during the past 12 months.

The 1999 survey results show a more positive picture than the 1998 results—more counties reported successful strategies in 1999 and fewer counties reported implementation problems with most CalWORKs requirements and rules. The majority of counties agree that funding is not a current problem in most service areas other than Stage 2 and Stage 3 child care, although finding the capacity in their counties for adequate service delivery, especially for child care and transportation, is of concern to many.

This report summarizes results from the 1999 ACIS. RAND will conduct a final ACIS in the fall of 2000.

These all-county surveys are only one component of RAND's Statewide CalWORKs Evaluation. A parallel report on implementation, *Welfare Reform in California: State and County Implementation of CalWORKs in the Second Year*, combines these ACIS results with information from interviews in 6 focus counties and 18 follow-up counties and from reviews of official documents and the secondary literature to give a richer description of the implementation of CalWORKs through summer 1999. Additional field work in the focus counties and less intensive visits to the larger number of follow-up counties will yield even richer characterizations of the implementation of CalWORKs in a third report to be released in February 2001. Finally, RAND will release reports in October 2000 and 2001 based on a parallel analysis of the impact of CalWORKs.

Acknowledgments

This report was made possible by the cooperation of all 58 county welfare departments in California, who completed the 1999 All-County Implementation Survey (ACIS). We thank the individuals who were generous with their time and took responsibility for ensuring the completion of the questionnaire. In addition, we are grateful to Denice Dotson, Marlene Pascua, Inslee Pitou, Kay Riley, Althea Shirley, and Mark Woo, who took time from their busy schedules to thoroughly review a draft of the questionnaire. Finally, thanks to our sponsor agency staff for coordinating internal and external CDSS review, which provided additional helpful input on the draft questionnaire.

At RAND, we are grateful to Survey Research Group (SRG) colleagues Kirsten Becker, who assisted with the design of the questionnaire; Linda Daly, who typed the questionnaire; to Patricia Frick, who set up the record management system and mailed out the survey materials and letters; to Ellyn Bloomfield, who followed up with the counties and kept track of survey progress; to Carole Berkson, who oversaw receipt and processing of incoming questionnaires; to Tom Bogdon, who helped to input the survey data quickly for the programming team; and to Shaoling Zhu, who prepared the data files for analysis. We would also like to thank RAND colleagues Sue Hosek and Bob Schoeni, who provided reviews and helpful comments on this draft.

Finally, a document such as this emerges because of the dedicated behind-the-scenes efforts of secretaries and publications staff members. They have handled the time pressures with grace and charity. Secretarial assistance was provided by Ann DeVille and Christopher Dirks. We are also grateful to the staff of RAND's Publications Department who worked on this document under a tight schedule. They include Betty Amo and Benson Wong.

Glossary

ACIS	RAND's All-County Implementation Survey
ADP	Alcohol and Drug Programs
AFDC	Aid to Families with Dependent Children
APP	Alternative Payment Provider
CalWORKs	California Work Opportunity and Responsibility to Kids Act of 1997
CBO	Community-based organization
CDSS	California Department of Social Services
CW	Combined Worker
CWD	County Welfare Department
EDD	Economic Development Department
FBO	Faith-based organization
GAIN	Greater Avenues for Independence (training program)
JTPA	Job Training Partnership Act
MOU	Memorandum of Understanding
PRWORA	Personal Responsibility and Work Opportunity Reconciliation Act of 1996
REB	CDSS Research and Evaluation Branch
RFP	Request for Proposal
SIP	Self-Initiated Program (of education)
SRG	RAND's Survey Research Group
TANF	Temporary Assistance to Needy Families
WIA	Workforce Investment Act
WtW	U.S. Department of Labor Welfare-to-Work grants
WTW	Welfare-to-Work programs

1. Introduction

Background

Continuing California's tradition of county administration of welfare programs, California's implementation of welfare reform—the California Work Opportunity and Responsibility to Kids (CalWORKs) program—granted considerable discretion to the state's counties in designing their welfare programs. Areas of county discretion included:

- Designing welfare-to-work (WTW) activities and services;
- Determining what activities to allow toward work requirements and whom to exempt from work requirements and for how long;
- Deciding what form collaboration should take among agencies and the private sector to provide training and support services and to identify jobs;
- Deciding what programs should be implemented to provide needed substance abuse and mental health services, child care, transportation, and domestic abuse assistance;
- Designing job retention and community service programs;
- Providing assistance for families transitioning off aid; and
- Providing public input to CalWORKs planning.

In addition, individual counties are responsible for the implementation of both the statewide changes and the county-specific plans. Counties were under tight time pressures to design a system to deliver the services that would move recipients into the work force and then to self-sufficiency within the statutory time limits. Counties are subject to financial sanctions for failure to meet federal participation requirements and can receive fiscal incentives for a percentage of grant savings due to exits from aid, work, and diversion. After the initial period of planning and the focus on enrollment and activities such as Job Club, which are part of the early stages of CalWORKs participation, during 1999 counties have begun to modify and refine their programs and to add components such as post employment services and community service jobs.

Objectives

This RAND report describes the results of a survey to track ongoing implementation of CalWORKs. The survey was conducted as part of a legislatively mandated independent evaluation of CalWORKs. The California Department of Social Services' (CDSS's) Request for Proposal (RFP) for the independent evaluation included a requirement for an annual county implementation survey to be conducted by mail "to determine the problems encountered, resolutions reached, and innovations created by the counties." The RFP listed specific aspects of administering CalWORKs that needed to be included in the first survey. Finally, the RFP required a county response rate of at least 80 percent.

Through a collaborative process with CDSS Research and Evaluation Branch (REB) staff, other CDSS staff, other state agencies, and representatives from several county welfare departments, RAND developed a questionnaire in September and early October of 1998. After analyzing those results and conducting further fieldwork, the 1999 ACIS was somewhat modified to expand the topics covered. Another review by state and local stakeholders helped finalize the content of the questionnaire. The 1999 survey was mailed September 29, and 50 counties had returned completed questionnaires by November 1. All 58 had replied by November 16, resulting in a 100 percent response rate for the second consecutive year.

Research Methods

Several considerations have guided the design of the 1999 All-County Implementation Survey (ACIS). First, the evaluation was more mature. When the survey was first fielded in 1998, it represented the first data collection task of the RAND CalWORKs evaluation, which started in September 1998. The contract called for a draft report on the survey results by January to provide early feedback to a variety of state and local stakeholders. Given the tight time frame, ACIS design took place before project staff had completed a first round of visits to counties selected as focus counties by CDSS.

For the second ACIS the situation was different. We had completed a first round of fieldwork and were in the process of conducting a second round of key informant interviews throughout 6 focus and 18 follow-up counties participating in the evaluation. Based on this fieldwork experience we knew that a number of issues had changed and that some CalWORKs components had become more routinized while others were now early in the implementation process. We wanted the survey to reflect current issues but also to facilitate comparison over time. We tried to incorporate into the ACIS some questions that we were pursuing in the field component of the process evaluation. Finally, we needed to hold down the size of the survey to minimize burden on the counties, and so several questions were dropped in order to make room for others.

Second, because the responses from each county were to again be published, we had to anticipate that counties would be unwilling to address some topics on the record.

Third, we knew that experiences among the counties were likely to vary, just as other characteristics of population, geography, and local government vary throughout California. This survey is the only part of the evaluation that enables us to collect data from all 58 of California's counties. It collects information on their perceptions of the context in which implementation is proceeding and on its progress. As such, it is an important tool for gathering information to help understand and interpret the differences we observe in administrative caseload and indicator data at the county level.

Fourth, the survey was to be conducted by mail with telephone follow-up. This field approach required a standardized questionnaire suitable for self-administration and a reasonable period of time to permit counties to respond.

Sample

The 1999 ACIS sample, like the 1998 survey, consisted of county welfare agency representatives. The 1998 list was updated before mailing in 1999. The addressee was the CalWORKs program director or the county welfare department (CWD) director when no CalWORKs program director had been appointed.

In addition, in 1999 a completely separate survey module was administered with the directors of non-CWD Alternative Payment Providers (APP) on the topic of child care. The results from that separate module are discussed in Chapter 7 of the report, *Welfare Reform in California: State and County Implementation of CalWORKs in the Second Year.*[1]

---

[1]Klerman, Jacob Alex, et al. *Welfare Reform in California: State and County Implementation of CalWORKs in the Second Year.* Santa Monica, Calif.: RAND, MR-1777-CDSS, 2000.

4

Survey Questionnaire[2]

During the summer of 1999, RAND staff developed the survey materials in collaboration with CDSS REB staff and reviewers from other state agencies and the counties. The evaluation coordinators from the evaluation's focus counties also reviewed the draft questionnaire. Topics were drawn from the list in the CDSS evaluation RFP and from topics that were clearly of importance throughout the state as implementation proceeded. Questions focused on:

- CWD organizational models for staffing, interagency arrangements, and provision of services;
- Caseloads, staffing, and resources;
- Success and problems, innovative strategies and programs; and
- The context in which implementation was occurring.

Mail-Out and Follow-Up

On September 29, 1999, survey packets were mailed to all counties, using priority mail service. The packets included a cover letter explaining the purpose of the survey and that responses would be published, the questionnaire, answers to questions frequently asked about the survey, and a brief overview of the RAND CalWORKs evaluation. A postage-paid envelope pre-addressed to RAND was included with the questionnaire.

One week after the initial mail-out, a follow-up letter was mailed to all counties as a "thank you" and reminder of the date for return of completed questionnaires (October 20).

Telephone reminders to the CalWORKs county contact in counties that had not yet returned the questionnaire began a week before the return date. These calls were intended to confirm that the questionnaire had been received and would be completed and returned. The calls typically involved a brief voice mail message or very brief conversation to answer any questions or ensure that the questionnaire had reached the appropriate person to complete it. Several questionnaires were remailed following these calls, and revised contact information was updated in the survey records management database.

Only one-third of the counties returned the questionnaire by the early due date. By November 1, 50 questionnaires had been returned and further telephone

---

[2]A copy of the questionnaire can be found in the Appendix.

follow-up and remailings of the questionnaire boosted the response rate to 100 percent by November 16.

Plans for Next Year's ACIS

Based on our original proposal and our experiences this year in designing and implementing the ACIS, we plan to again expand the survey sample beyond the welfare agency in each county to include other agencies and community-based organizations (CBOs) that receive CalWORKs funding, contract with the welfare agency, or serve CalWORKs participants.

We will also use the ACIS to address issues and themes that arise in the focus county and follow-up county fieldwork conducted during 2000 and to assess the generalizability of the interview findings.

Organization of This Document

The remaining sections present the results of the 1999 ACIS. Section 2 discusses organizational issues including how the counties have staffed their CalWORKs programs, their interagency arrangements, what services are available and how they are provided, and what information counties have available about various categories of participants. Section 3 describes caseload, staffing, capacity, and funding changes during the past year. Section 4 summarizes reports from the counties about their successes and about continuing challenges and problems with CalWORKs program requirements and rules. Section 5 summarizes our findings and identifies several themes that have emerged. An appendix contains a copy of the survey materials mailed to the counties. In addition, the detailed results can be accessed for each county and separate groups of counties using a new database query facility provided at our CalWORKs web site: http://www. rand.org/CalWORKs/AllCounty.

2. CalWORKs Program Organization and Provision of Services

The 1998 ACIS documented the variation in implementation patterns across the state.[1] We found that the counties varied in how they organized their programs, what services were available, and what problems and successes they experienced in the first year of the program. These are characteristics worth monitoring over time. This year we asked for more specifics about county welfare department (CWD) staffing, interagency relationships, what services are offered and how they are provided, and what kinds of information counties have about their various categories of CalWORKs participants. The findings are not intended to provide detail on implementation but to shed some light on the variation across the state and on where there is and is not consensus among the counties.

Structure and Organization of CalWORKs Programs

In the 1998 ACIS we found that extensive organizational changes were accompanying CalWORKs implementation across the state. In 1999 we also asked about the structure and organization of CalWORKs programs, concentrating on general models for CWD CalWORKs staffing, interagency arrangements, and provision of services.

CWD Staffing

Staffing has been an important issue in most counties. During our site visits in the counties, key informants discussed staff shortages, need for training, labor problems, and how job functions of former eligibility and GAIN staff have changed with the shift from AFDC to Temporary Assistance to Needy Families (TANF).[2] We asked the counties to report on several staffing models, including whether they have combined the job of eligibility and employment/Welfare to Work (WTW) caseworker, reclassified caseworker positions, co-located eligibility and employment staff, decided which personnel conduct CalWORKs orientation in their county, or outsourced their CalWORKs WTW operations. Figure 2.1

---

[1]Ebener, Patricia A., and Jacob Alex Klerman. *Welfare Reform in California: Results of the 1998 All-County Implementation Survey.* Santa Monica, Calif.: RAND, MR-1052-CDSS, 1999.
[2]See Chapter 5 of Klerman et al., 2000.

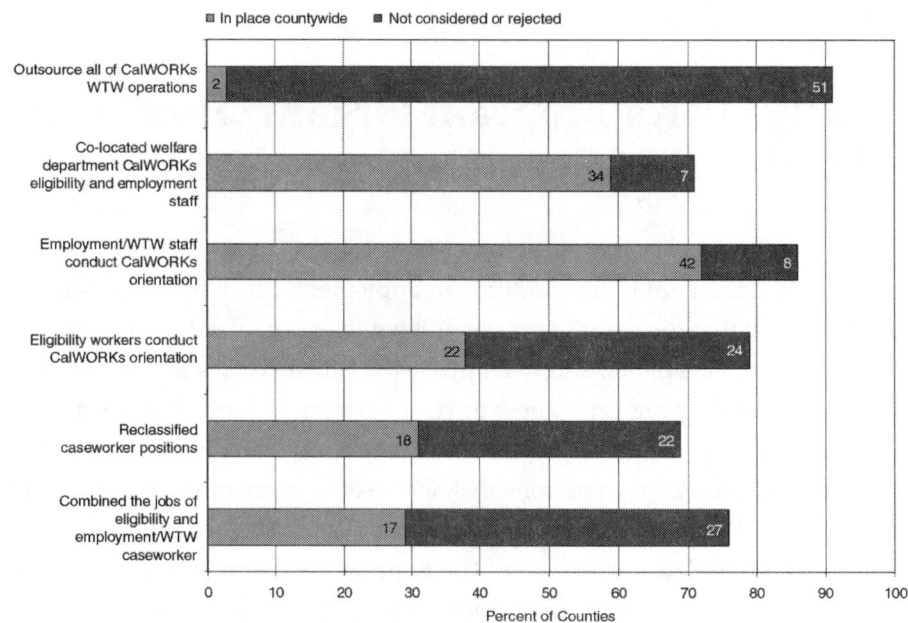

Figure 2.1—CalWORKs Staffing Models
(For the other models, see Figure 2.2)

shows that the counties still vary considerably in approaches to staffing CalWORKs. It shows the number of counties that have each model in place countywide and the number that have not considered or considered and decided not to adopt each model. The names of counties that have these models in place countywide are shown in Table 2.1.

The only widespread consensus is that wholesale outsourcing of WTW operations has not been popular. About 60 percent report that they have co-located their eligibility and employment staff, while few report rejecting this model. About 70 percent conduct CalWORKs orientation using employment/welfare to work staff. However, about 40 percent use eligibility workers for CalWORKs orientation while an almost equal number have decided not to adopt this model. Sixteen counties are using both categories of workers. Thirty percent reported that reclassification of caseworkers had taken place or that they had combined the jobs of eligibility and WTW caseworkers. Greater percentages reported that these two models had not been considered or were considered, but not adopted.

Figure 2.1 also shows that not all counties are accounted for. As shown in Figure 2.2, in some counties, one or more of these models have been adopted but only

Table 2.1

Counties with CalWORKs Staffing Models in Place Countywide

	Outsource all of CalWORKs welfare to work operation	Co-located welfare department CalWORKs eligibility and employment staff	Employment/WTW staff conduct CalWORKs orientation*	Eligibility workers conduct CalWORKs orientation*	Reclassified caseworker positions	Combined the jobs of eligibility and employment/WTW caseworker
Alameda			✓	✓		
Alpine		✓	✓			✓
Amador		✓	✓			
Butte				✓	✓	
Calaveras			✓		✓	
Colusa		✓	✓			
Contra Costa		✓			✓	✓
Del Norte		✓	✓		✓	✓
El Dorado		✓	✓	✓		
Fresno		✓		✓		
Glenn		✓	✓			
Humboldt		✓	✓			
Imperial		✓	✓			
Inyo		✓	✓	✓		
Kern	✓	✓	✓	✓		
Kings			✓		✓	
Lake		✓	✓	✓		✓
Lassen		✓	✓	✓		✓
Los Angeles		✓				
Madera			✓	✓		
Marin*			✓	✓		
Mariposa			✓			
Mendocino			✓			
Merced			✓			
Modoc			✓			
Mono		✓	✓			
Napa		✓	✓	✓		✓
Orange		✓		✓		✓
Placer			✓			
Plumas		✓	✓			✓
Riverside			✓			
Sacramento			✓		✓	✓
San Benito		✓			✓	✓
San Bernardino			✓			
San Diego				✓		
San Francisco		✓	✓		✓	✓
San Joaquin			✓		✓	
San Luis Obispo					✓	✓
San Mateo		✓	✓		✓	✓
Santa Barbara					✓	
Santa Cruz		✓	✓	✓	✓	
Shasta		✓		✓		
Sierra		✓	✓			
Solano*		✓	✓	✓	✓	✓
Sonoma		✓	✓	✓		
Stanislaus		✓				
Sutter*			✓	✓		
Tehama		✓	✓			
Trinity			✓			
Tulare		✓	✓		✓	
Tuolumne		✓				
Ventura		✓		✓	✓	✓
Yolo			✓	✓		
Yuba	✓	✓	✓		✓	✓

*Teams/combinations of workers conduct orientation.

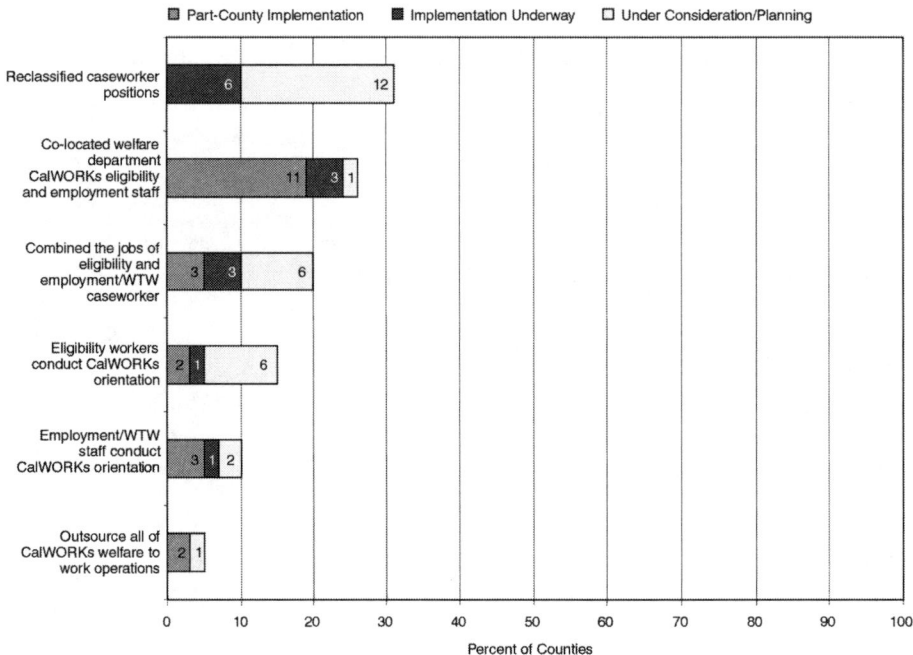

Figure 2.2—Ongoing Implementation of Staffing Models

partially, in others their implementation (countywide or part-county) is currently underway and in others still under consideration.

For example, while 31 percent of counties have completed reclassification of caseworker positions, and another 38 percent have not considered reclassification or decided not to adopt this option, still another 31 percent have reclassification underway or under consideration at this time. The extent of partial or ongoing implementation and consideration of staffing changes suggests that a significant number of counties are still exploring alternative staffing models and that further changes should be expected.

Models of Interagency Coordination

The CalWORKs program clearly calls for interagency coordination and cooperation in a number of areas. Key informants described a variety of ways in which the CWDs have tried to accomplish this, many without much prior experience in working with other agencies.[3] Co-locating CalWORKs staff with staff from partner agencies, interagency case management, and pooling of funds for services delivery are among the models being used. The 1999 ACIS asked all

---

[3]Klerman et al., 2000.

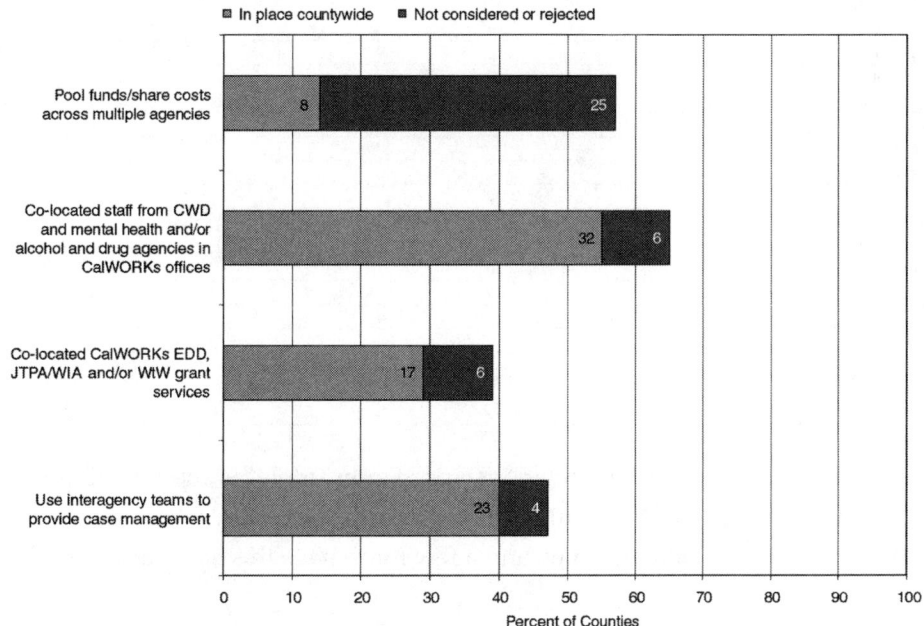

11

counties to report on their use of these approaches. The results are summarized in Figure 2.3. The names of the counties that report having adopted these interagency models countywide are shown in Table 2.2.

The most frequently adopted approach on a countywide basis is co-locating behavioral health and CWD CalWORKs staff, which just over half the counties reported in place countywide and few have so far ruled out. Forty percent of the counties have in place using interagency teams to provide case management and fewer than 10 percent have so far ruled out this model. Countywide interagency co-location between CWD CalWORKs and behavioral health department or EDD/JTPA/WtW Grant providers was reported by almost 30 percent of the counties and few have decided not to adopt this approach. About 40 percent have decided not to adopt or not considered the option of pooling funds or sharing costs across agencies. Much more common, as we discuss below, is the practice of Memorandum of Understanding (MOU) or other interagency arrangements for referring CalWORKs clients directly from CWDs to agencies with funding for specific services.

Figure 2.3 shows that quite a few counties have yet to fully implement or even to consider interagency options. From 40 to 60 percent, depending on the specific approach, are still dealing with the consideration or implementation of these

Figure 2.3—CalWORKs Interagency Models

Table 2.2

Counties with Interagency Models in Place Countywide

	Pool funds/share costs across multiple agencies	Co-located staff from welfare and mental health and/or alcohol and drug agencies in CalWORKs offices	Co-located CalWORKs EDD, JTPA/WIA and/or Welfare to Work grant services	Use interagency teams to provide case management
Alameda	✓			
Alpine				✓
Amador			✓	
Butte	✓			
Colusa				✓
Contra Costa		✓		
El Dorado		✓		✓
Glenn	✓	✓	✓	✓
Humboldt				✓
Inyo		✓		
Kern	✓	✓	✓	✓
Lake		✓	✓	
Lassen		✓	✓	
Madera		✓		
Marin	✓	✓	✓	
Mariposa		✓		✓
Mendocino		✓		
Modoc	✓	✓		
Mono			✓	✓
Monterey		✓		
Napa		✓	✓	✓
Orange		✓	✓	
Placer		✓		✓
Plumas				✓
Riverside		✓		
Sacramento		✓		
San Benito				✓
San Francisco	✓	✓	✓	✓
San Joaquin		✓	✓	
San Luis Obispo				✓
San Mateo		✓		✓
Santa Cruz		✓	✓	✓
Sierra		✓		✓
Siskiyou		✓	✓	✓
Solano		✓		
Sonoma	✓		✓	✓
Stanislaus		✓	✓	
Sutter		✓		
Tehama		✓		✓
Trinity				✓
Tulare		✓		
Ventura		✓	✓	✓
Yolo		✓	✓	
Yuba		✓		✓

models of interagency working relationships. For example, as shown in Figure 2.4, another 45 percent of the counties have partially co-located CWD and EDD/JTPA, WtW Grant personnel, and a few more have this approach under consideration.

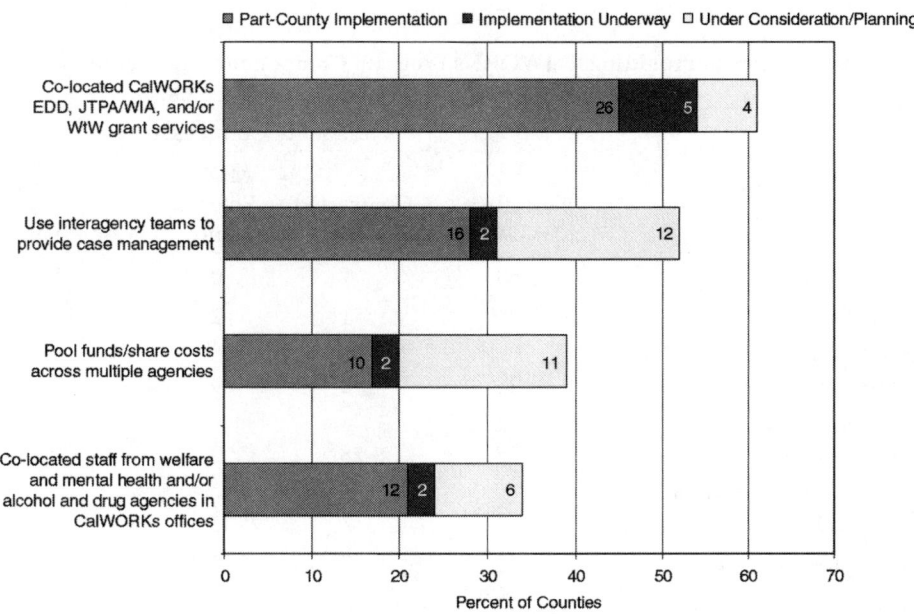

Figure 2.4—Interagency Models

Likewise, in addition to the 40 percent of counties with countywide interagency case management for CalWORKs clients, 28 percent have interagency case management in some of their CalWORKs offices and 21 percent are considering this approach. Two points are evident from these results. First, further changes in organizational approaches should be expected. Second, even when counties report similar implementation approaches they may have different implications in terms of the scale of implementation so far completed.

Outsourcing

As noted above, few counties have outsourced their entire WTW operation. But outsourcing is popular with the counties in a variety of service areas. They accomplish this in two ways: first, by contracting with community organizations to provide the service and second, by arrangements with other county agencies funded directly to provide such services, e.g., mental health and substance abuse treatment. In other areas the counties tend to provide services directly. However, as shown in Table 2.3, often a variety of mechanisms are used to provide CalWORKs program components and services for special populations.

Table 2.3

Approaches to Providing CalWORKs Program Components and Services

	Number of Counties			
Program Components	Directly by CWD Only	Contracted Only	MOU/ Referral Only	Combination
CalWORKs orientation	53	1	0	4
Job assessment	28	11	2	16
Screening and referral for domestic abuse services	28	2	9	18
Stage 1 child care administration	25	28	2	3
Screening and referral for mental health services	22	7	13	16
Post employment services	22	7	5	23
Screening and referral for substance abuse	20	7	13	18
Job Club	20	16	7	15
Stage 3 child care	1	25	28	3
Stage 2 child care	4	24	24	5
Services for work barriers				
No high school diploma	2	11	39	6
Limited literacy skills	1	7	34	14
No work experience	13	9	6	29
Chronic health problem/ disability	1	5	28	10
Language barrier	12	7	13	30
Legal problems	6	6	20	11
Remote location/lack of transportation	22	7	3	13
Substance abuse treatment	1	13	35	8
Mental health treatment	2	13	34	9
Educational services	2	9	34	12
Domestic abuse services	2	12	31	11
Vocational training	2	8	33	13
Services targeting refugee families	9	7	2	9
Services targeting non–English-speaking families	13	7	6	24

Services Provided

Another variation across the counties is in the types of services offered. While all counties provide all the basic components of CalWORKs such as orientation, Job Club, and job assessments, they vary somewhat in terms of other services, e.g., for specific work barriers such as health and legal problems, services for refugee families, and transportation. Table 2.4 shows the variability in services provided.

Table 2.4

Services Not Provided

Program Components	Counties Where Services Are Not Provided	
	Number	Percentage
CalWORKs orientation	0	0
Job assessment	0	0
Screening and referral for domestic abuse services	0	0
Stage 1 child care administration	0	0
Screening and referral for mental health services	0	0
Post employment services	2	3
Screening and referral for substance abuse	0	0
Job Club	0	0
Stage 3 child care	1	2
Stage 2 child care	1	2
Services for work barriers		
No high school diploma	0	0
Limited literacy skills	2	3
No work experience	0	0
Chronic health problem/disability	11	19
Language barrier	5	9
Legal problems	15	26
Remote location/lack of transportation	10	17
Substance abuse treatment	0	0
Mental health treatment	0	0
Educational services	1	2
Domestic abuse services	1	2
Vocational training	2	3
Services targeting refugee families	29	50
Services targeting non–English-speaking families	7	12

Home Visits

During key informant interviews with our focus and follow-up counties we learned that quite a few counties have begun to make home visits as part of their CalWORKs program. In the ACIS we asked all the counties to report on whether and when they make home visits for new applicants, participants about to be sanctioned, and participants who have had a sanction applied. Their replies are summarized in Table 2.5.

Few counties make home visits to applicants before eligibility determination, and the few that do mostly do so on a selective or a pilot basis. However, altogether 34 counties are making home visits either before or after applying sanctions, though few do so in all cases. Several that do not indicated that they are planning such programs for the future. Home visits to prevent or follow up on sanctions are in use throughout the state by all sizes of county though large- and medium-size counties are slightly overrepresented in this group.

Thirty-five counties reported that they make home visits for other purposes in some or all cases. Most frequently named purposes were for fraud prevention or detection (9 counties); intensive case management or families with special barriers (8 counties); follow-up on "no shows" (6 counties); and when transportation, remote location, or illness make it impossible for clients to visit CalWORKs offices (6 cases).

Table 2.5

Use of Home Visits by Counties

	In All Cases	Pilot Project or Subset of Cases	Never or Almost Never
New applicants before eligibility determination	9%	14%	72%
Before sanctions are applied	15%	29%	50%
After sanctions have been applied	14%	41%	38%
Other	24%	36%	19%

Statistical Reporting

CalWORKs caseloads can be divided into many categories of participants, the status of which are useful to monitor for planning, operations, and evaluation purposes. As implementation proceeds we were interested in learning about the extent to which the counties have been monitoring the various categories of participants. One question in the 1999 ACIS asked how many counties receive regular (defined as at least quarterly) statistical reports on different categories of participants. The categories are shown in Figure 2.5 along with the number and percent of counties that have statistical reporting on each category.

Statistical reporting is widespread. Not surprisingly given the monthly WTW 25 report (instituted as of the July 1999 reporting period as the survey was being filled out), 98 percent of counties have regular statistical reporting on the participants enrolled in welfare to work activities, employed, using subsidized child care, and enrolled in WtW grant program services. At the opposite end of the continuum 57 percent have no statistical reporting on participants approaching 60-month time limits and 26 percent have no regular statistics on participants approaching the 18/24-month time limit, items that are not included in the WTW 25. Across the various categories, it appears that large and medium counties are more likely to lack statistical reporting than small counties.

The ACIS question asked about statistical reporting for 20 categories of participants and diversions. Twelve counties indicated that they receive statistical reporting for all 20 categories. Twenty-two reported that they have reporting on all except 1 or 2 categories, and another ten counties lack reporting for only 3 to 5 categories of participants. Only two counties lack reporting for over half of the categories of participants included.

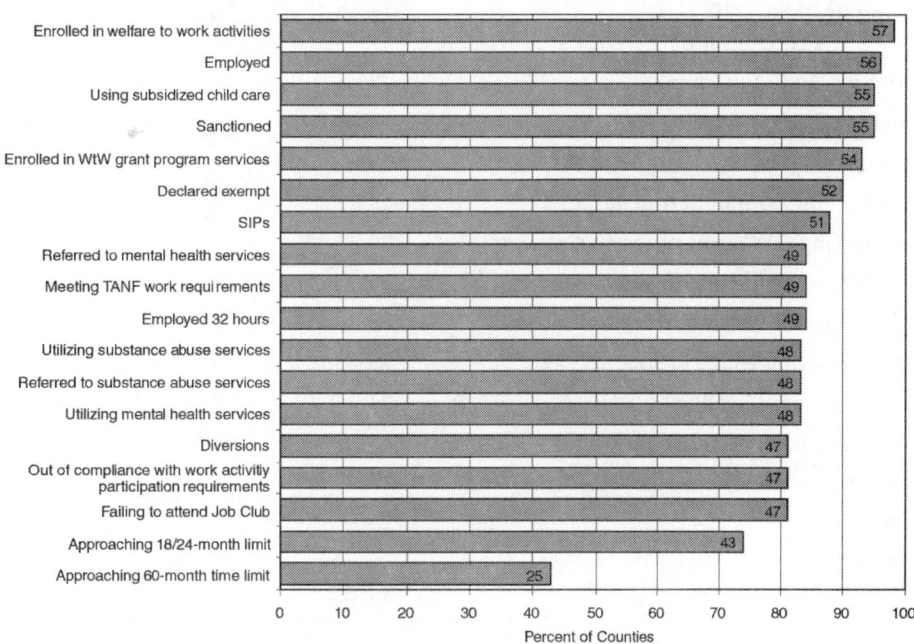

Figure 2.5—Widespread Availability of Statistical Reports

18

The ACIS also asked about the level of management—county level senior management, district managers, and supervisors—at which statistical reporting was available. Table 2.6 shows the percentage of counties with regular statistical reporting at the three levels of management by category of reporting. It is clear from this table that statistical reporting is most widespread at the supervisor level of management. Only a few categories, such as diversions, are more likely to be available at the senior management level than at the supervisor level. It is worth noting that the numbers for district manager level are lower probably because many small counties do not have district managers rather than because they receive fewer statistical reports in the counties where they exist.

Table 2.6

Statistical Reporting by Level of CalWORKs Managers

	Number of Counties		
	Senior Management	District Managers	Supervisors
Enrolled in welfare to work activities	41	33	44
Employed	43	32	42
Employed 32 hours	25	26	35
Meeting TANF work requirements	26	24	37
Using subsidized child care	30	28	37
Failing to attend Job Club	16	23	41
Out of compliance with work activity participation requirements	18	24	37
Sanctioned	35	32	40
Approaching 18/24-month limit	18	22	35
Approaching 60-month time limit	7	8	16
Enrolled in WtW grant program services	26	29	38
Referred to mental health services	26	24	36
Referred to substance abuse services	25	24	36
Referred to domestic violence services	19	23	35
Utilizing mental health services	24	22	33
Utilizing substance abuse services	23	22	32
Utilizing domestic abuse services	14	18	30
SIPs	25	25	41
Declared exempt	30	25	39
Diversions	32	21	24

Within counties the most typical pattern is for statistical reports to be available at multiple levels of management. Only ten counties limit reporting to a single level, either supervisors or senior management, and most of these are small counties where there are fewer levels of management. In six counties reports on some categories of participants are received at one level and reports on other categories are received at another level.

3. Changes in County Caseloads, Staffing, and Resources

In addition to asking about CalWORKs program organizational differences among counties the ACIS asked counties to report on changes in their caseloads, staffing, and resources. Differences among the counties and changes over time may help explain differences in outcomes and implementation experiences. The ACIS included questions about changes in caseload and staff increases during the past 12 months. It also repeated the 1998 ACIS question about capacity and funding resources for a variety of services.

Caseload Declines

Twenty-three counties, 40 percent of the 58 counties, reported that the per-worker caseloads of both eligibility workers and employment/welfare to work (WTW) workers have declined over the past 12 months. Only two counties reported increases in caseloads for both types of workers and eight counties reported that caseloads had remained about the same for most eligibility and WTW workers. The remaining twenty-two counties that replied to this question had experienced some caseload increase, mostly for WTW workers, and some decrease. Sixteen counties, 28 percent of the total, reported increases in the caseloads of most WTW workers. Increases occurred disproportionately among the medium-sized counties. However, in most of the counties where increases in WTW caseloads occurred, there were decreases in the eligibility workers' caseloads during the same period. Only six counties reported eligibility worker caseload increases.

Staffing Increases

Most counties increased their CalWORKs staffing during the past 12 months. Forty-four counties increased the number of eligibility and/or WTW caseworkers and 36 added supervisory and/or management staff. Just over half, 33, hired at both levels. Eight counties did not add CalWORKs staff during the past year. Most of the increase in caseworkers was accomplished from a combination of filling vacancies and hiring for new positions, while hiring for new positions was the means most often used to add supervisory/management staff. Large counties were more likely and small counties less likely to report increases in their CalWORKs staff.

Other Resources

Services Capacity

In both years of the survey we asked the counties to indicate any shortfalls, current or anticipated, in capacity to deliver a variety of different services from child care to training. Figure 3.1 displays the counties' 1999 responses for capacity shortfalls.

It shows off hours and weekend child care, transportation, mildly ill and infant child care topping the list of services with current capacity shortfalls. These same four areas ranked at the top of the list in 1998. Half or more of the counties report current or anticipated capacity shortfalls for ten of the seventeen service areas shown on Figure 3.1.

Shown at the bottom portion of the chart are the seven areas where a majority of counties, about 70 percent or more, report no shortfall.

Counties vary somewhat in current shortfalls based on size. For example, 91 percent of small counties report current capacity shortfalls for off hours/ weekend child care compared to 62 percent and 71 percent for medium and large counties, respectively. While almost 50 percent of small counties report current

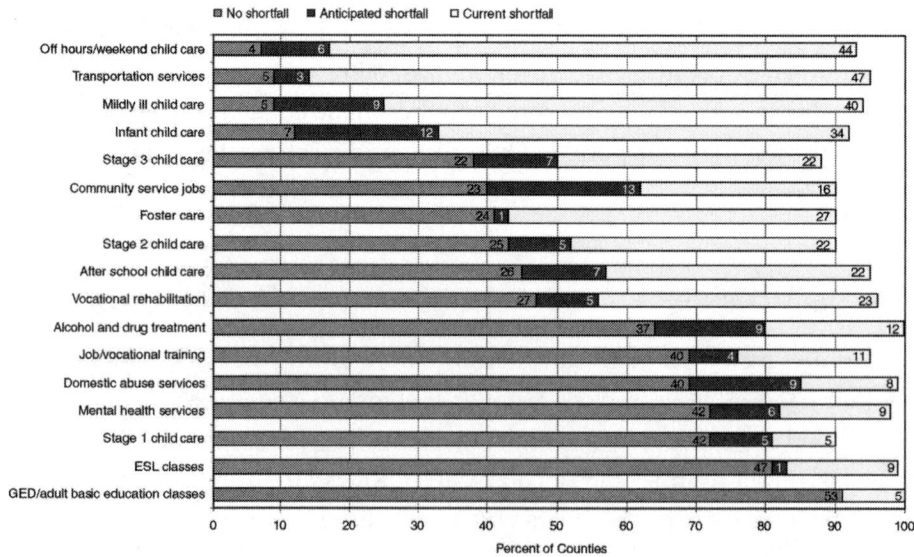

Figure 3.1—Capacity Shortfalls

capacity shortfalls for community service, only 19 percent of medium and 7 percent of large counties do so. Finally, close to 90 percent of both small and medium counties report current capacity shortfalls for transportation, while little over 60 percent of large counties report such shortfalls.

Figure 3.2 shows the differences in current and anticipated capacity shortfalls for 1998 and 1999 for children's services. What is somewhat different between the two years is that fewer counties report in 1999 that they anticipate future shortfalls for a variety of services especially those for children. For half or fewer counties, with the exception of mildly ill child care, the numbers anticipating shortfalls in 1999 are significantly fewer than in 1998. The numbers reporting current shortfalls are little changed between 1998 and 1999.

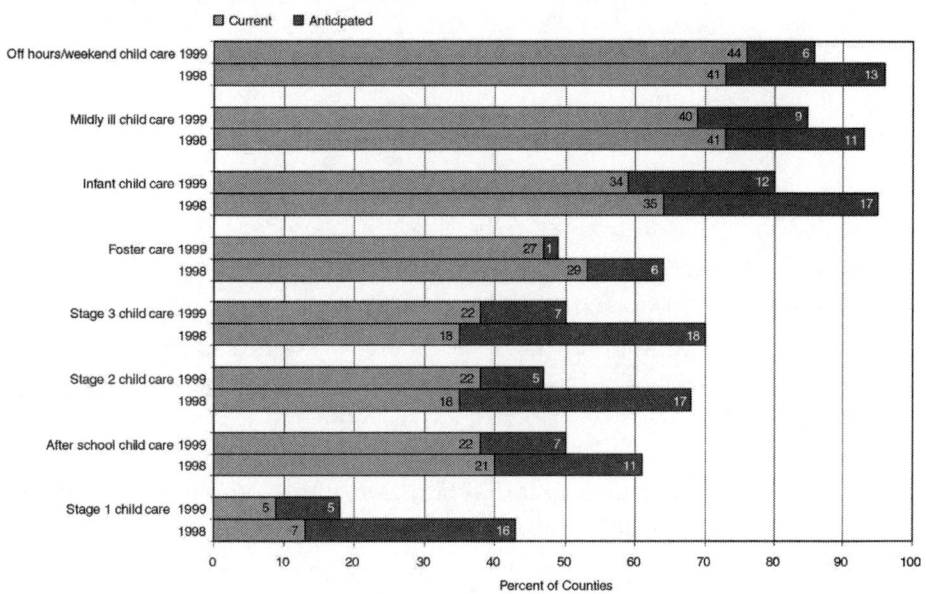

Figure 3.2—Capacity Shortfalls—Children's Services, 1998 vs. 1999

Services Funding

The ACIS also asked the counties to report on funding shortfalls to pay for the same services. Figure 3.3 shows the 1999 results. The result is somewhat different from the capacity story.

Most counties report only a few service areas with current funding shortfalls. Stage 2 and Stage 3 child care top the list with 35 and 38 counties respectively reporting current funding shortfalls for these services. Those who report current

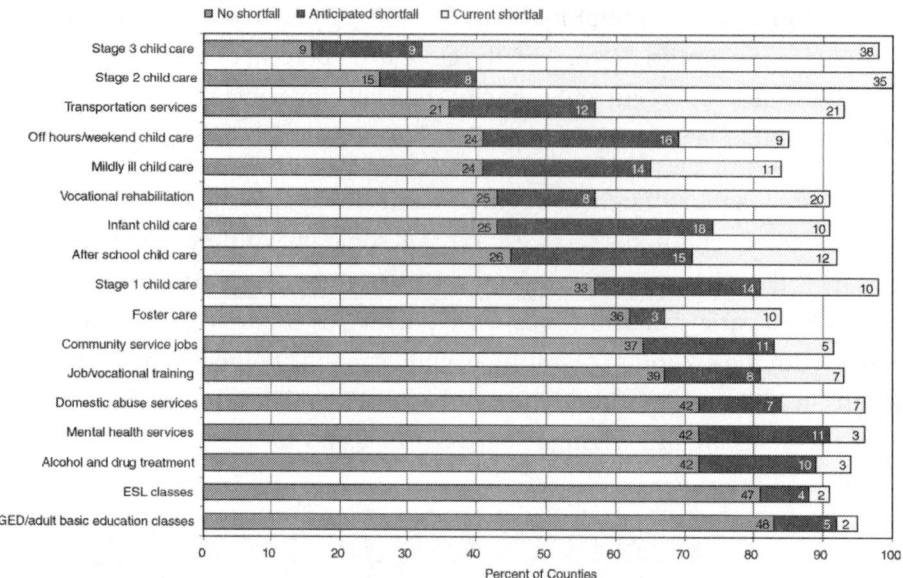

Figure 3.3—Funding Shortfalls

or anticipated shortfalls do so most in the children's services area. Approximately 40 percent of both small and medium counties report current funding shortfalls for vocational rehabilitation whereas only 14 percent of large counties report such funding shortfalls. In contrast with the capacity shortfall picture, large counties are more likely to report child care funding shortfalls than small counties.

The trend is mixed. For Stage 1, 2, and 3 child care, more counties report current shortfalls in 1999 than in 1998. For several other children's services, more counties anticipate shortfalls than in 1998. About 30 percent now anticipate shortfalls in funding for off hours, mildly ill, infant, and after school child care. For job training and other supportive services such as treatment, fewer counties report current or anticipated shortfalls in 1999 but more report current shortfalls for job/vocational training, ESL classes, GED/basic education services, and transportation. These comparisons are shown in Figure 3.4.

Another way to assess the resource limitations that some counties face is to examine the number of counties that respond to having shortfalls in both capacity and funding. Looking across capacity and funding figures, we find that current shortfalls in both are most common for Stage 2 and Stage 3 child care, transportation services, and vocational rehabilitation.

Of the 17 included services, the average number of reported current shortfalls in either or both capacity and funding per county is 7. Seventeen percent of the

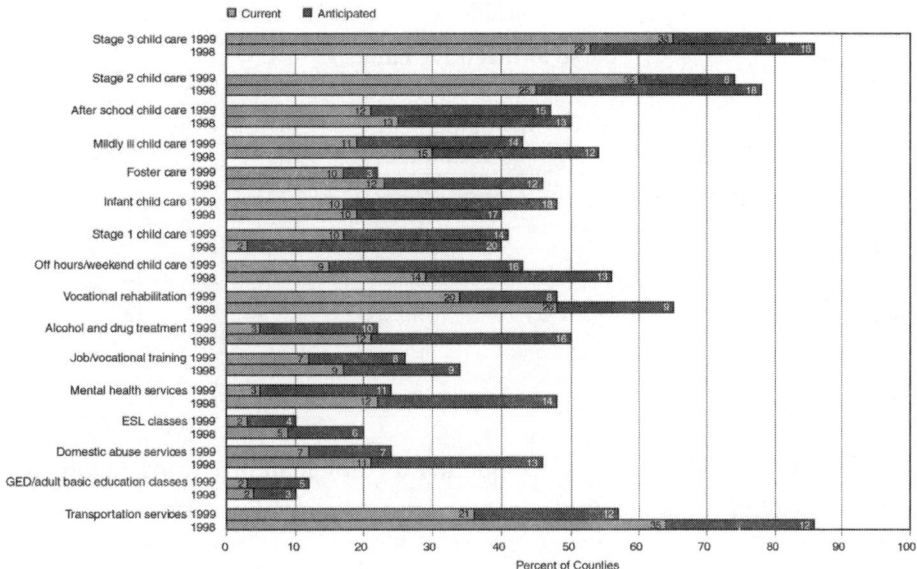

Figure 3.4—Funding Shortfalls, 1998 vs. 1999

counties report 3 or fewer, while 27 percent of the counties report having current shortfalls in 10 to 15 of the 17 service areas.

Small- and medium-size counties report more capacity and funding shortfalls than the large counties. Thirty percent of small counties and 33 percent of medium-size counties have current shortfalls in most service areas, compared with 14 percent of the large counties. Small counties are also underrepresented among those with few shortfalls. Only 9 percent of small counties compared with 21 and 23 percent of large and medium counties reported fewer than 4 service areas with current shortfalls. These results demonstrate the cross-county variation in resources available for CalWORKs and related services.

Incentive Funds

All counties have received their incentive or bonus funds for last year's performance in lowering caseloads and falling aid payments due to earnings diversion. This funding provides added resources that the counties can use in a variety of ways. According to the ACIS responses 43 percent of the counties have yet to allocate these funds. As shown on Table 3.1, among those that have, most are using the funds for new programs. Counties could name multiple purposes in response to the question about how their funds would be used. Those planning to use the funds for new programs named a variety of different

Table 3.1

Use of Incentive Funds

Use of Funds	Number of Counties	Percentage of Counties
Not yet planned/allocated	25	43
New programs	25	40
Reserve	8	14
New staff	8	14
Capital improvements	6	10
Other	10	17

programs. Those mentioned most frequently include loan programs, health and behavioral health programs, transportation, and employment services.

4. Counties' Views of CalWORKs Success and Challenges

The ACIS is the only component of the Statewide CalWORKs Evaluation that provides qualitative information about the implementation experiences of all 58 counties. This section provides the results from questions that asked the counties to assess how well various aspects of their CalWORKs programs are working and what challenges remain.

Where possible we compare their responses with those from the 1998 ACIS.

Successful Strategies to Address Implementation Challenges

Providing feedback to stakeholders on successful implementation strategies is one of the purposes of the ACIS. This year's questionnaire included a list of 18 implementation challenges (see Table 4.1) and asked that counties report on those for which they believed they had particularly successful strategies. The definition of success was left to the counties. One county, Plumas, noted in response that it is involved with strategies in many of the areas listed but it had no data or impressions of which were more effective than others. Few counties have systematically evaluated interventions or program modifications designed to address implementation problems. Nonetheless the inventory of strategies provided by the counties in response to this question does illustrate the range and variation in strategies being adopted to address implementation problems such as noncompliance, transportation assistance, and monitoring program outcomes. Table 4.1 lists each of the implementation challenges included in the ACIS question and the counties that described strategies for addressing them in their ACIS reply.

Half or more of the counties indicated that they had successful strategies for the following implementation challenges:

- Working with the community (e.g., community based organizations [CBOs], faith based organizations [FBOs], employers, and business groups);

Table 4.1

Strategies for Implementation

Strategy	Alameda	Alpine	Amador	Butte	Calaveras	Colusa	Contra Costa	Del Norte	El Dorado	Fresno	Glenn	Humboldt	Imperial	Inyo	Kern	Kings	Lake	Lassen	Los Angeles	Madera	Marin	Mariposa	Mendocino	Merced	Modoc	Mono	Monterey	Napa	Nevada
Implementing sanctions			✓				✓	✓													✓		✓						
Detecting and prosecuting fraud						✓	✓		✓						✓	✓			✓		✓								
Implementing a diverse program						✓	✓		✓							✓	✓		✓									✓	
Ensuring transitional services for families leaving old			✓						✓						✓	✓			✓	✓	✓		✓				✓		
Increasing participation among 2-parent families						✓	✓					✓			✓	✓				✓	✓		✓						
Increasing compliance with required CalWORKs activities	✓					✓		✓	✓						✓	✓			✓	✓	✓		✓	✓					✓
Encouraging use of post employment/job retention services	✓								✓						✓		✓		✓	✓			✓	✓					
Promoting economic development	✓		✓				✓		✓	✓					✓	✓	✓		✓		✓		✓	✓					
Monitoring program performance	✓								✓						✓	✓			✓	✓			✓	✓					
Increasing utilization of subsidized child care						✓		✓	✓						✓	✓			✓		✓		✓				✓		✓
Improving computer services			✓			✓		✓	✓	✓					✓	✓			✓	✓	✓		✓				✓		
Providing transportation assistance			✓			✓	✓	✓	✓	✓					✓	✓	✓		✓				✓						
Communicating rules to non-English-speaking clients			✓			✓	✓		✓	✓					✓	✓		✓	✓		✓		✓	✓					
Home visits to prevent or remedy sanctions	✓	✓				✓	✓		✓	✓					✓	✓	✓		✓				✓				✓		✓
Coordinating with WtW grant providers	✓								✓	✓					✓	✓			✓				✓	✓			✓		
Linking participants with job training program	✓		✓			✓	✓			✓		✓			✓				✓	✓	✓		✓	✓			✓	✓	
Working with the community	✓		✓				✓	✓		✓		✓			✓	✓			✓	✓	✓		✓	✓			✓	✓	
Mental health, domestic abuse, or substance abuse services	✓		✓			✓	✓	✓	✓	✓		✓		✓	✓	✓	✓	✓	✓	✓			✓	✓			✓		✓

Table 4.1 (Continued)

	Orange	Placer	Plumas	Riverside	Sacramento	San Benito	S. Bernardino	San Diego	San Francisco	San Joaquin	S. Luis Obispo	San Mateo	Santa Barbara	Santa Clara	Santa Cruz	Shasta	Sierra	Siskiyou	Solano	Sonoma	Stanislaus	Sutter	Tehama	Trinity	Tulare	Tuolumne	Ventura	Yolo	Yuba
Implementing sanctions	✓	✓							✓	✓	✓				✓				✓										
Detecting and prosecuting fraud	✓	✓				✓	✓			✓	✓				✓				✓				✓						
Implementing a diverse program	✓	✓								✓	✓					✓			✓	✓	✓					✓		✓	
Ensuring transitional services for families leaving old	✓					✓		✓	✓	✓	✓			✓	✓												✓		
Increasing participation among 2-parent families	✓	✓		✓		✓				✓	✓				✓				✓	✓						✓	✓		
Increasing compliance with required CalWORKs activities				✓				✓		✓	✓	✓		✓	✓												✓		✓
Encouraging use of post employment/job retention services	✓	✓	✓		✓					✓	✓	✓	✓	✓	✓											✓	✓	✓	
Promoting economic development	✓	✓		✓		✓				✓	✓								✓	✓	✓	✓			✓				
Monitoring program performance	✓	✓		✓		✓	✓			✓	✓	✓	✓					✓	✓	✓	✓	✓							
Increasing utilization of subsidized child care	✓		✓			✓			✓	✓	✓	✓	✓	✓					✓	✓	✓						✓		✓
Improving computer services	✓	✓		✓	✓	✓				✓		✓							✓	✓	✓	✓	✓		✓				
Providing transportation assistance	✓			✓		✓				✓	✓	✓	✓	✓		✓			✓	✓		✓	✓			✓	✓		✓
Communicating rules to non–English-speaking clients	✓	✓		✓	✓	✓			✓	✓	✓	✓	✓	✓					✓	✓	✓						✓		✓
Home visits to prevent or remedy sanctions			✓			✓		✓	✓	✓	✓	✓			✓				✓	✓	✓		✓			✓	✓		✓
Coordinating with WtW grant providers	✓	✓		✓	✓	✓	✓	✓	✓	✓	✓		✓	✓	✓				✓	✓	✓		✓		✓	✓	✓	✓	
Linking participants with job training program	✓	✓	✓	✓	✓	✓		✓		✓	✓	✓	✓	✓				✓	✓	✓	✓	✓	✓		✓		✓	✓	
Working with the community	✓	✓		✓	✓	✓			✓	✓	✓	✓		✓	✓			✓	✓	✓	✓	✓	✓				✓	✓	
Mental health, domestic abuse, or substance abuse services	✓	✓	✓	✓	✓	✓			✓	✓	✓	✓		✓	✓				✓	✓	✓	✓	✓	✓		✓	✓	✓	

- Identifying needs and providing services for participants with mental health, domestic abuse, or substance abuse problems;

- Home visits to prevent or remedy sanctions;

- Coordinating with WtW grant providers;

- Linking participants with job training programs; and

- Communicating CalWORKs program requirements and rules to non–English-speaking applicants and participants.

Fewer than half indicated successful strategies in the following areas of implementation:

- Implementing sanctions;

- Detecting and prosecuting fraud;

- Increasing participation rates among two-parent families;

- Implementing diversion programs;

- Promoting economic development;

- Encouraging use of post employment/job retention services;

- Monitoring program performance outcomes;

- Providing transportation assistance;

- Ensuring continuing child care, MediCal, and/or Food Stamps for families leaving aid;

- Increasing utilization of subsidized child care;

- Improving computer systems; and

- Increasing compliance with required CalWORKs activities (e.g., limiting "no shows").

We compared the 1999 responses with those from 1998 for the implementation challenges included in both years' questionnaires and found, as shown in Figure 4.1, increased numbers of counties reporting successful strategies in 1999 compared to 1998 for six out of seven implementation challenges. This result suggests that the counties may be making progress in their efforts to address implementation problems.

Strategies to Deal with Implementation Challenges

Thirty-seven, mostly large- and medium-size counties (see Table 4.1) provided descriptions of strategies for working with the community, including CBOs,

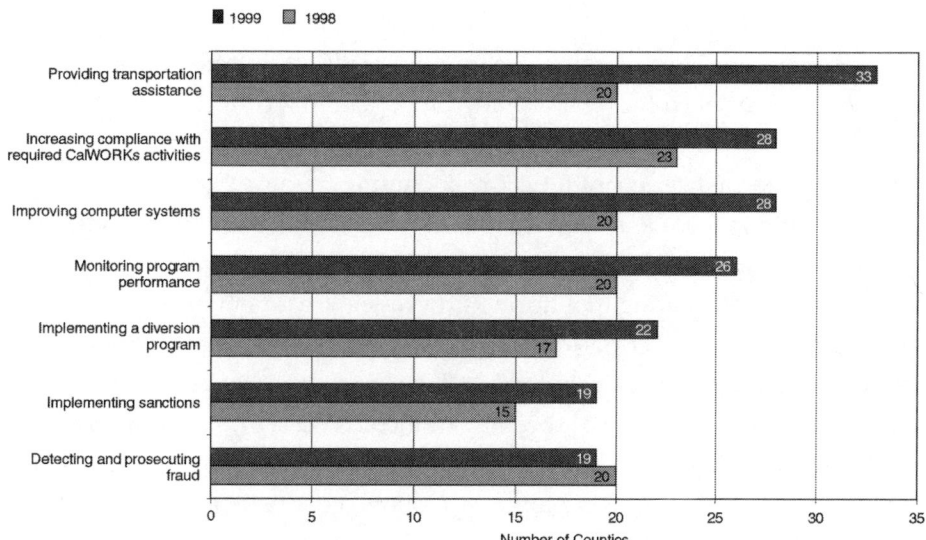

Figure 4.1—More Counties Report Successful Implementation Strategies in 1999

FBOs, employers, and business groups. The underrepresentation of the small counties may be because of the shortage of CBOs and employers in some areas. For example, Colusa County noted that working with the community is a big problem for them because they have few employers and no CBOs.

Among the strategies named for working with the community were outreach, collaboration, and/or regular contacts with CBOs, FBOs, employers, and business groups to gather input, jointly plan, provide oversight, and educate various groups about CalWORKs. Two reported co-locating CalWORKs staff in CBO facilities. Four reported specifically on working with FBOs. For example, in San Bernardino County FBOs are doing outreach to CalWORKs households that have received a first sanction. Other counties reported that co-case managing, One Stops, other programs such as CalJOBs, and their history of collaboration facilitate working with the community. Other strategies reported include contracting with CBOs, planning activities, and even the creation of a new division within the CWD to work with the communities.

Identifying needs and providing services for mental health, domestic abuse, and substance abuse is another area of implementation where most counties reported successful strategies. We were somewhat surprised that 40 counties had successful strategies to describe, given the low rate of referral and utilization of these services by CalWORKs clients.[1] The most frequently named strategy was

---

[1]Klerman et al., 2000.

co-location of staff from the alcohol and drug programs (ADPs), mental health (MH), and domestic abuse services areas with CalWORKs staff. However, from the 20 descriptions of co-location provided it is clear that co-location means different things in different places. Co-located behavioral health and domestic abuse staff perform a variety of functions including training CWD staff; providing information about services to CalWORKs clients at orientations, workshops, and seminars; screening and assessments; referral and liaison with service providers, including monitoring progress in treatment; providing therapeutic services; and co-case managing with CalWORKs staff. Other less frequently named strategies included contracting to provide outreach with clients in the community, use of specially trained CWD staff, staff training, contracting with CBOs to provide services, and efforts to identify problems "up front" or during orientation. In Monterey County, county behavioral health staff provide a "stress management module" and describe services available as part of CalWORKs orientation. Several counties named multiple strategies being used in combination, and one, Fresno, reported that it had recently completed an evaluation of how it was providing substance abuse services for its clients.

Twenty-eight counties described strategies for meeting transportation problems. Small counties were again underrepresented in this group relative to their percentage of the total. Transportation problems can be especially acute in rural areas and while 8 small counties were included in the 28, it is not surprising that most small counties did not report successful strategies in this area. Colusa indicated that transportation problems are one of their worst barriers. About 10 counties said the CWD itself provides or contracts to provide rides for CalWORKs clients; another 10 said they had arranged for the expansion of routes or extension of hours for public bus service to improve access for CalWORKs clients. Twelve counties reported on a variety of subsidy programs to provide for repairs, purchase of vehicles, loans, and payment of automobile insurance for participants.

For other implementation challenges far fewer counties claimed they had successful strategies. For example, only 12 described successful strategies for implementing sanctions and most of these involved strategies to avoid sanctions, such as outreach with noncompliant households and use of incentives and disincentives. These counties had few cases sanctioned, while others indicated that they had been active in processing sanctions. Solano County reported that it has strategies designed to avoid the need for additional sanctions but also provides training for staff on noncompliance and expects timely imposition of sanctions.

Encouraging use of post employment and job retention services has also proven difficult, and many counties are currently focused on this component of their programs. This is evident from the ACIS responses as few counties offered specific strategies and several indicated that they were planning this program or hiring new staff or piloting or considering other options. Two reported that job retention hot lines were in use, one provides incentives such as gift certificates to those who remained employed for a certain period of time, and several talked about the need for outreach to remind clients that post employment services are available and to encourage their use.

Increasing participation rates among two-parent families can be another challenging area, although some counties that responded to this question indicated that the participation rate for two-parent families was not a problem for them. The successful strategies described by the counties fell into three areas: identifying the needs of both parents; prioritizing two-parent families for services, such as referral to WtW grant program; and providing additional services such as intensive case management, family- versus participant-focused services, and services addressing cultural issues.

Implementing diversion programs (in which a potential recipient receives a lump sum payment rather than becoming a welfare recipient) has also posed problems for some counties that report that few clients make use of this program. Others such as Fresno, Lake, Orange, and Sonoma have had successful experiences (e.g., clients not coming back on aid) with diverting cases although they had not diverted large numbers. Some described their approach as utilizing flexible criteria and/or a case by case approach. San Luis Obispo reported that workers take the time to fully explore options with their clients.

The ACIS also asked the counties to review a related list of CalWORKs program components and to select five that were the strongest elements of their program and five that needed the most improvement or modification in order to meet CalWORKs goals. The program components from which they selected are shown in Figure 4.2. They are ranked according to the number of counties that named each as among the five strongest elements of their CalWORKs program. Also shown is the number of counties naming the element among the five needing most improvement.

34

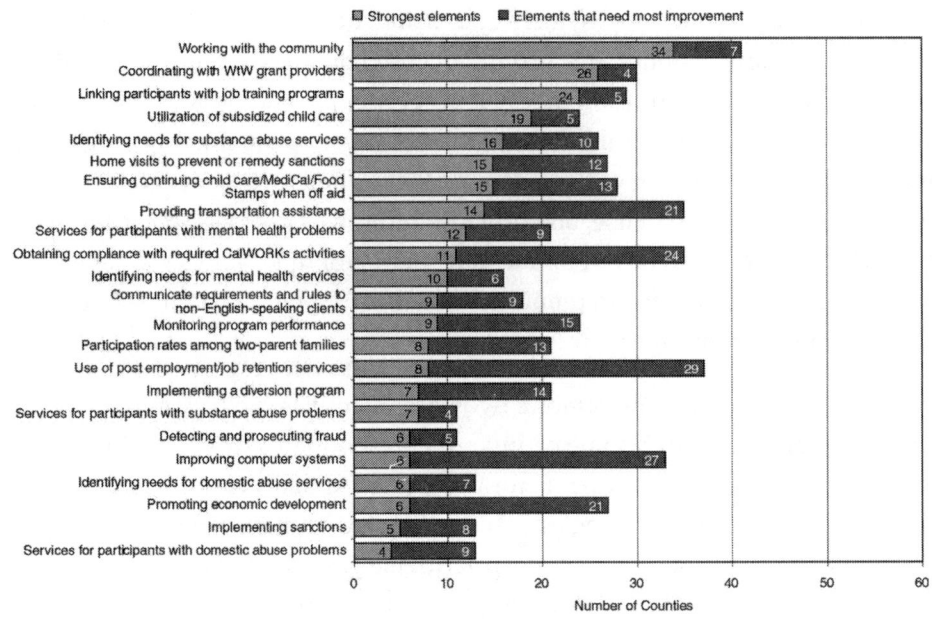

Figure 4.2—CalWORKs Program Elements

This figure points out the variation around the state in experiences with CalWORKs implementation. Among 23 program elements, only 2 were selected by half or more of the counties. Thirty-four rated working with the community as among their strongest CalWORKs program elements, and exactly half rated use of post employment/job retention services among those needing most improvement. Often as many counties rated an element among the strongest as rated it among the weakest. For example, nine counties reported that communicating CalWORKs rules to non–English-speaking participants was one of the 5 strongest elements in their CalWORKs program while another nine rated that element among the 5 needing most improvement. The lack of consensus shown in these results suggests that the counties have had quite different experiences with CalWORKs implementation, a finding that is not surprising given the diversity among the 58 counties and their CalWORKs populations. These results roughly agree with the prior table that showed more counties reporting successful strategies for elements similar to those at the top of the ranking in Table 4.1, and fewer counties with successful strategies for the program elements at the bottom of the ranking, such as implementing sanctions.

Implementing the Rules

A year ago California counties were in the midst of learning the new CalWORKs requirements and interim regulations and putting the program into place. A year later we were anxious to determine whether there have been changes in how the counties view the CalWORKs program rules and requirements. We again asked the counties to review a long list of the program's requirements and rules and to indicate whether these rules were presenting temporary or ongoing problems or were not a problem at this time. The 1999 list somewhat overlapped with the list presented in 1998. The results are fairly consistent with significant agreement among the counties that most rules are not posing implementation problems. Figure 4.3 presents the list ranked by the percent of counties reporting that it is not a problem at this time. Among the 20 rules listed in the 1999 questionnaire, a majority of counties indicated that 11 of the 20 were not a problem in their counties at this time. Between 45 and 50 percent said that another 5 of the rules were not posing a problem at this time. Only 2 requirements, coordinating of three stages of child care and monitoring/ reporting on county performance outcomes were reported by a majority of the counties to pose ongoing problems at this time. These requirements also topped the list in the 1998 survey.

Of the 20 CalWORKs program requirements and rules included in the ACIS list, the average number posing ongoing problems per county is 6. Twenty-two percent of the counties report 3 or fewer, while 12 percent report that 10 to 15 of

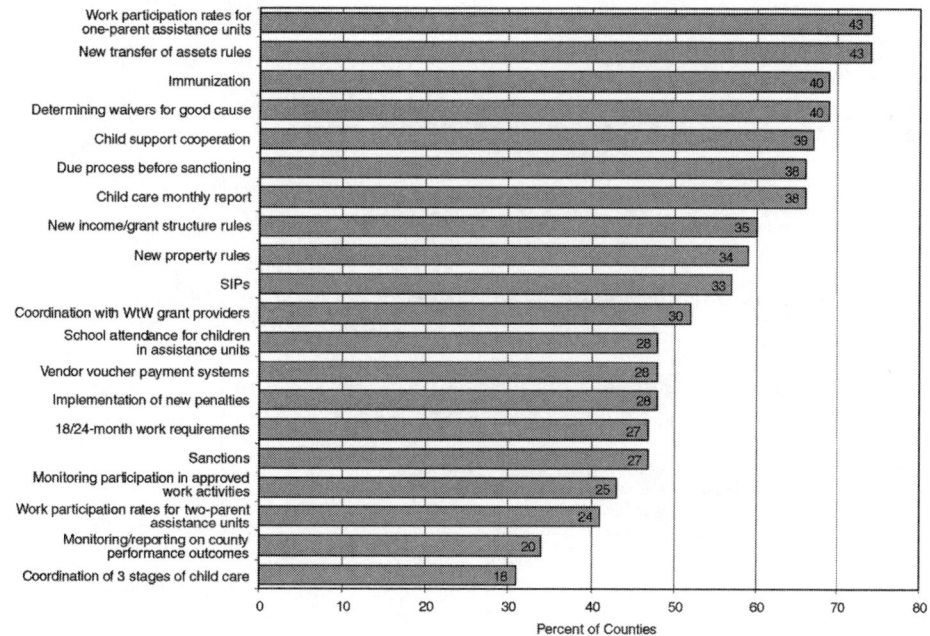

Figure 4.3—Rules Least Likely to Present Implementation Problems

36

the CalWORKs rules are presenting ongoing problems. While small counties reported more shortfalls in resources than large counties, small counties reported fewer problems with CalWORKs requirements and rules than did large counties. Only 4 percent of small counties had ongoing problems with many requirements compared with 14 percent of large counties. Forty percent of small counties reported 3 or fewer problem areas compared with only 7 percent of large counties. Among medium counties the results are more mixed. Nineteen percent were at the high end with 10 or more problem areas while 14 percent were at the low end with fewer than 4 ongoing problem areas related to CalWORKs requirements and rules.

Not surprisingly, the number of counties reporting start-up or transitional problems has declined significantly from last year. In some cases transitional problems appear to have been resolved and in others to have become ongoing. Figure 4.4 shows the difference between 1998 and 1999 for the CalWORKs rules that were most likely to be a problem in 1998. Over time, some turn out to be posing ongoing problems in more counties and others in fewer. For example, the number of counties that say coordinating the three stages of child care presents an ongoing problem increased from 21 to 35 counties over the past year; while the number of counties reporting that work requirement rates for two-parent families presented an ongoing problem decreased from 35 to 27.

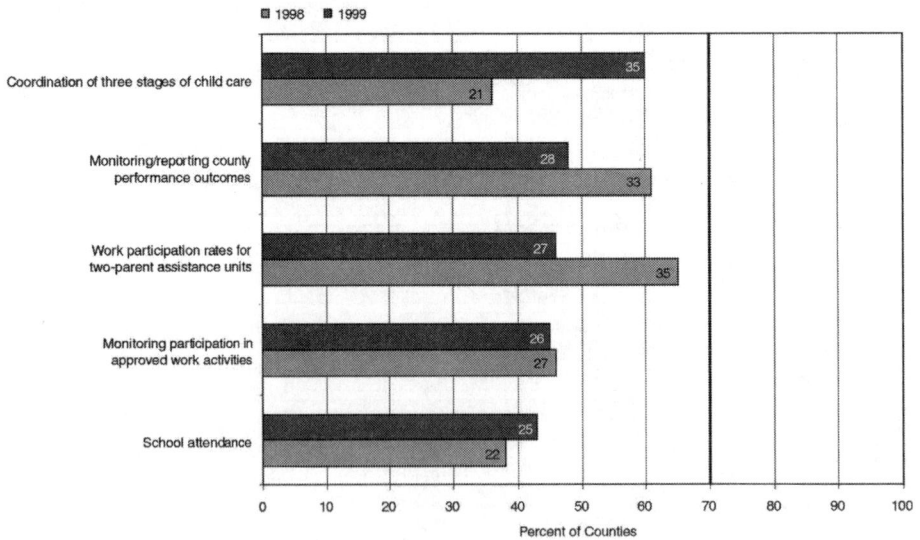

Figure 4.4—Rules Most Likely to Present Implementation Problems, 1998 vs. 1999

Two-Parent Family Participation Requirements

Meeting work participation requirements for two-parent families has been an ongoing concern at the state level, though the experience at the county level has varied depending on how many two-parent families are in the caseload and what their employment experience has been. Immigrant and refugee families make up a significant portion of the two-parent family caseload. These families may be at higher risk for poor job histories because of language difficulties, poor educational attainment, and cultural barriers. This year the ACIS questionnaire asked about the work barriers and other issues that are problems for two-parent families in the CalWORKs caseload. The counties were asked to select up to three barriers or challenges, from a list of fourteen,[2] that are particularly prevalent or difficult for three groups: two-parent refugee families, two-parent immigrant families and two-parent non-refugee, non-immigrant families. Table 4.2 shows the barriers named most frequently and the number of counties that associated them with each group. It is not surprising that socio-cultural and language barriers topped the list, but there are some notable differences. Almost twice as many counties name limited literacy skills as a problem for immigrant families compared with refugee families and non-refugee, non-immigrant

Table 4.2

Two-Parent Participation Barriers

	Number of Counties		
	Two-Parent Refugee Families	Two-Parent Immigrant Families	Two-Parent Non-refugee, Non-immigrant Families
Socio-cultural barriers	23	25	7
Language barriers: obtaining employment	21	32	0
Limited literacy skills	12	26	14
Language barriers: understanding/using CalWORKs	11	12	1
No work history/experience	3	3	28
Lack of transportation	2	6	17
No high school diploma/GED	1	3	16
Legal problems	1	3	12
Substance abuse problems	0	0	30

[2]No high school diploma, limited literacy skills, no work history/experience, mental health problems, substance abuse problems, domestic abuse problems, chronic health problems/disability in family, children ill or with special needs, language barriers: obtaining employment, language barriers: understanding and using CalWORKs, socio-cultural barriers, legal problems, remote location, lack of transportation.

38

families. The counties named quite different barriers for non-refugee, non-immigrant families.

Factors That Hinder and Facilitate Implementation

As noted above, counties have different structural and organizational approaches to CalWORKs programming and report differences in implementation successes and problems. We asked counties to review a list of characteristics associated with communities and CWDs and to indicate which have hindered and which have facilitated implementation of CalWORKs, or whether they have had no effect to date. The results, ranked by those most likely to hinder implementation, are shown on Figure 4.5 for the 1999 survey list of characteristics. This chart shows a fair amount of agreement among the counties on what hinders and what facilitates implementation. At the top of the chart are the characteristics that almost all counties agree are hindering implementation. At the bottom are those where a large majority agree that they facilitate implementation. The supply of entry-level jobs appears to hurt in about half the counties and to help in the other half. Similarly welfare department staff training, experience, and culture are factors on which counties differ on whether they hinder or facilitate implementation.

In general the counties seem to be more positive about the influence of characteristics of their economies and the CWD on implementation in 1999 than they were in 1998. Among eight characteristics included on the survey both

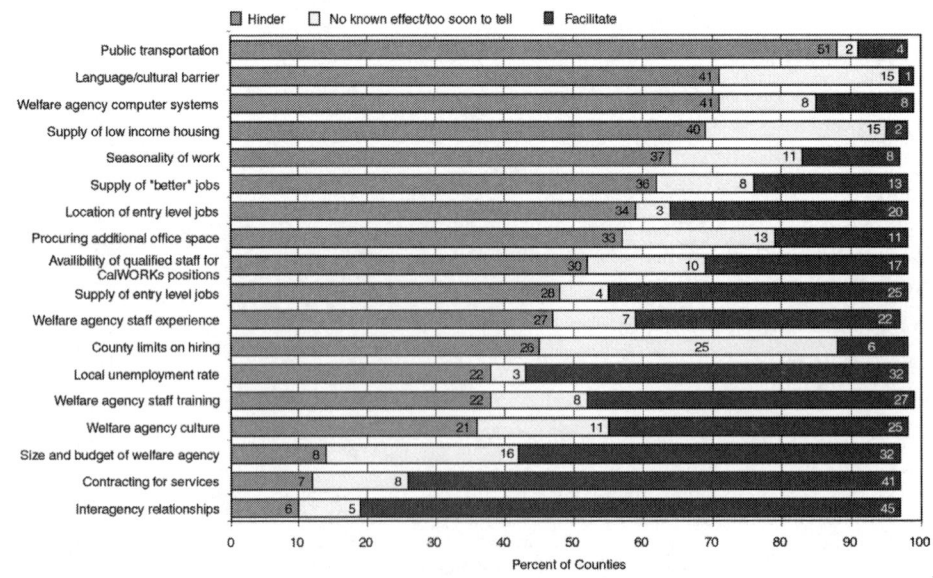

Figure 4.5—Factors That Hinder and Facilitate Implementation

years, more counties reported that they facilitated implementation in 1999 than in 1998, for all except one factor—county welfare staff experience. For this factor, the number that reported it hinders implementation increased from 17 in 1998 to 27 in 1999. The comparison between years is shown on Figure 4.6.

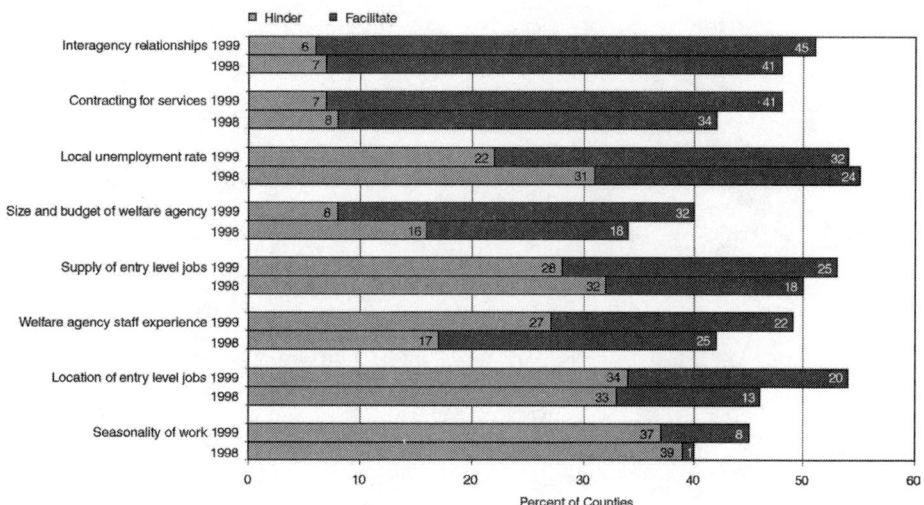

Figure 4.6—Factors That Hinder and Facilitate Implementation, 1998 vs. 1999

5. Conclusions

In general, California counties reported a more favorable view of CalWORKs in 1999 compared to 1998. Fewer reported problems with CalWORKs requirements and rules, and fewer CWD and economic factors hinder implementation. More counties reported they had successful implementation strategies in a variety of areas. Most indicated that they have regular statistical reporting on the status of the various categories of CalWORKs caseloads. Over the past year, caseload declines were more common than increases, although 16 counties did report increases in the caseloads of most employment/WTW staff. In spite of declines in numbers of cases, most counties added CalWORKs staff. Over half hired both caseworkers and supervisory management staff in what appears to be an effort to meet the increased workload for the remaining caseload. For example, half the counties have started to make home visits part of their CalWORKs program.

In most categories of CalWORKs services except Stage 2 and Stage 3 child care, few counties report current funding shortfalls. Looking at the capacity to provide services, most counties reported current or anticipated shortfalls in a variety of child care types, transportation, and community service jobs. Forty-three percent of counties have as yet unallocated incentive funds, and about 40 percent said they will use the funds for new programs. Our findings on CWD resources support the contention of many of our key informants that linking clients with needed services can be difficult if capacity is inadequate and requires increased staff in spite of caseload declines. The availability of funding including incentive funds suggests that if new programs and increased capacity can be developed, funding will not be a problem in the short term.

Organizational changes continue at CWD and interagency levels. Some models have become fairly common. For example, almost 60 percent now co-locate eligibility and employment/WTW CalWORKs staff. Fifty-five percent co-locate CWD CalWORKs staff and mental health or behavioral health department staff. Many other approaches are less widespread with as many counties rejecting an approach as have adopted it. About equal numbers provide Stage 1 child care via CWD as contract out this service. Many counties are using a combination of mechanisms including CWD staff, contracts with CBOs, and MOUs with other county agencies, to provide CalWORKs program components and services for work barriers.

Clearly the ACIS does not provide the context or the details of implementation that our key informant interviews and site visits provide in 6 focus and 18 follow-up counties participating in the evaluation. What the reports from 58 counties do provide is a broad picture of implementation statewide and a view of progress over time that other components of the evaluation cannot offer. Given the differences in approach, scope, and content of CalWORKs program components that the ACIS reveals, it is our conclusion that comparisons across counties must be made with caution when trying to explain differences in outcomes using implementation information provided in the ACIS.

We conclude from these data that implementation continues within a variety of staffing and interagency organizational models and that further organizational changes may be in store, especially in the use of home visits for pre- and post-sanction CalWORKs families and in the development of post employment/job retention and community service job programs.

As implementation continues, the counties face a number of remaining challenges that could affect their success in meeting CalWORKs goals. Among the frequently named program elements in most need of improvement were post employment/job retention services and obtaining compliance with required CalWORKs activities. Few had successful strategies to offer in these areas. Few had successful sanctions strategies. Few have yet to focus on monitoring progress of their caseload toward the 60-month lifetime limit.

We expect that the third ACIS in the summer of 2000 will provide another update on implementation progress and highlight the variation among counties and the ongoing challenges facing most counties.

Appendix

ACIS Questionnaire

Following is a replica of the 1999 All-County CalWORKs Implementation Survey that was sent to all 58 counties.

```
┌──────────────────────────────────────┐
│  LABEL HERE  –  COUNTY NAME           │
│              –  COUNTY ID             │
└──────────────────────────────────────┘
```

1999 ALL-COUNTY CalWORKs IMPLEMENTATION SURVEY

County contact person for follow-up/clarification of questionnaire responses:

Name: _____   Title: _____

Telephone: (____) _____   Fax: (____) _____

Office Use Only

Received	____ / ____	/ 99
TSC ID	____ / ____	/ 99
TSC	____ / ____	/ 99

Please use the enclosed pre-addressed return envelope to send this completed questionnaire and any enclosures to:

RAND

1700 Main Street
P.O. Box 2138
Santa Monica, CA 90407-2138

ATTN: Pat Ebener, M-18

Instructions for Completing this Questionnaire

- This questionnaire should be completed by the person directing the County's implementation of CalWORKs or his or her designee.

- There are no right or wrong answers to these questions. Please read the questions carefully and use your best judgment in selecting responses. If you find that some of the choices printed in the questionnaire do not allow you to describe the experience of your county adequately, please feel free to respond in your own words.

- Please mark response choices clearly.

- Feel free to add comments. Use additional space provided at the end of the questionnaire or add pages or other materials, whichever is easier.

- Specific instructions are provided for each question.

- Please return completed questionnaire no later than **October 20, 1999** to **RAND** ATTN: Pat Ebener, M-18, 1700 Main Street, P.O. Box 2138, Santa Monica, CA 90407-2138.

- Remember to enter contact information on the front cover and to enclose any supplemental materials.

- If you have any questions, please feel free to contact Pat Ebener, **RAND**, (310) 393-0411, x7905, or via email: pateb@rand.org, or Kirsten Becker, **RAND**, x6480.

1. There are several variations across counties in the structure and organization of their CalWORKs programs. This question is about how your county program is structured and organized.

STRUCTURE AND ORGANIZATION OF CalWORKs PROGRAM	In Place County Wide	In Place In Part of the County	Implementation Underway At This Time	Under Consideration/ Planning At This Time	Check Here If NOT Considered Or Rejected
	(Check One Box on Each Line)				
a) Co-located welfare department CalWORKs eligibility and employment staff...............	❏	❏	❏	❏	❏
b) Combined the jobs of eligibility and employment/welfare to work caseworker...........	❏	❏	❏	❏	❏
c) Co-located staff from welfare and mental health and/or alcohol and drug agencies in CalWORKs offices	❏	❏	❏	❏	❏
d) Co-located CalWORKs EDD, JTPA/WIA and/or Welfare to Work grant services................................	❏	❏	❏	❏	❏
e) Use interagency teams to provide case management.......................	❏	❏	❏	❏	❏
f) Outsource all of CalWORKs welfare to work operations.................	❏	❏	❏	❏	❏
g) Reclassified caseworker positions............................	❏	❏	❏	❏	❏
h) Pool funds/share costs across multiple agencies (not contracts)	❏	❏	❏	❏	❏
i) Eligibility workers conduct CalWORKs orientation	❏	❏	❏	❏	❏
j) Employment/welfare to work staff conduct CalWORKs orientation	❏	❏	❏	❏	❏
k) Other, please specify:........	❏	❏	❏	❏	❏

_____

2. There are also differences in how counties deliver components of their CalWORKs programs. This question is about whether your welfare department provides these components directly or outsources them and if so, to whom. Check the box on the far right if a component or service is not provided.

PROGRAM COMPONENTS	Directly by CalWORKs Agency	Through Welfare Dept. Contract with Nonprofit Provider	Through Welfare Dept. Contract with For Profit Provider	Referral/ MOU with Agencies Funded to Provide Service	OR, Check Here if Service Not Provided
How are these services provided?					
(Check All That Apply on Each Line)					
a) CalWORKs orientation	❑	❑	❑	❑	❑
b) Job Club	❑	❑	❑	❑	❑
c) Job assessment	❑	❑	❑	❑	❑
d) Vocational training	❑	❑	❑	❑	❑
e) Educational services	❑	❑	❑	❑	❑
f) Post employment services	❑	❑	❑	❑	❑
g) Stage 1 child care administration	❑	❑	❑	❑	❑
h) Stage 2 child care administration	❑	❑	❑	❑	❑
I) Stage 3 child care administration	❑	❑	❑	❑	❑
j) Screening and referral for mental health services	❑	❑	❑	❑	❑
k) Mental health treatment	❑	❑	❑	❑	❑
l) Screening and referral for substance abuse services	❑	❑	❑	❑	❑
m) Substance abuse treatment	❑	❑	❑	❑	❑
n) Screening and referral for domestic abuse services	❑	❑	❑	❑	❑
o) Domestic abuse services	❑	❑	❑	❑	❑
p) Services targeting refugee families	❑	❑	❑	❑	❑
q) Services targeting non–English-speaking families	❑	❑	❑	❑	❑

3. Throughout California, stakeholders are anxious to obtain feedback from counties on the innovative strategies and successes that have made CalWORKs implementation possible. Some counties have developed strategies they believe are particularly successful in supporting implementation of their CalWORKs programs. **Please indicate whether your county has found any of its strategies in the following areas to be particularly successful**. Check all that apply and provide a brief description of your strategy or program or attach an already existing description, whichever is easier.

❏ a) Communicating CalWORKs program requirements and rules to non–English-speaking applicants and participants

_____

❏ b) Linking participants with job training programs _____

_____

❏ c) Increasing compliance with required CalWORKs activities (e.g., limiting "no shows")

_____

❏ d) Increasing utilization of subsidized child care _____

_____

❏ e) Increasing participation rates among two-parent families _____

_____

❏ f) Home visits to prevent or remedy sanctions _____

_____

❏ g) Implementing a diversion program _____

_____

❏ h) Detecting and prosecuting fraud _____

_____

❏ i) Providing transportation assistance _____

_____

❏ j) Ensuring continuing child care, MediCal and/or Food Stamps for families leaving aid _____

_____

❏ k) Implementing sanctions _____

_____

❏ l) Working with the community (e.g., CBOs, faith based organizations, employers and business groups)

_____

❏ m) Coordinating with Welfare to Work grant providers _____

_____

❏ n) Improving computer systems _____

_____

❏ o) Monitoring program performance (e.g., of contractors, County CalWORKs employees, County's overall CalWORKs performance)

_____

❏ p) Identifying needs and providing services for participants with mental health, domestic abuse or substance abuse problems

_____

❏ q) Promoting economic development _____

_____

❏ r) Encouraging use of post employment/job retention services _____

_____

❏ s) Other, please specify: _____

_____

4. Which five of the program components listed in the box below would you select as the strongest elements of your CalWORKs program? Enter the letters corresponding to the program components you select.

☐ ☐ ☐ ☐ ☐

5. Which five of the program components listed in the box below are you least satisfied with, or believe need the most improvement or modification in order to meet your county's CalWORKs goals? Enter the letters corresponding to the program components you select.

☐ ☐ ☐ ☐ ☐

PROGRAM COMPONENTS	
A. Communicating CalWORKs program requirements and rules to non–English-speaking applicants and participants	L. Working with the community
	M. Coordinating with Welfare to Work grant providers
B. Linking participants with job training programs	N. Improving computer systems
	O. Monitoring program performance
C. Obtaining compliance with required CalWORKs activities	P. Identifying participants with needs for mental health services
D. Utilization of subsidized child care	Q. Identifying participants with needs for domestic abuse services
E. Participation rates among two-parent families	R. Identifying participants with needs for substance abuse services
F. Home visits to prevent or remedy sanctions	S. Providing services for participants with mental health problems
G. Implementing a diversion program	T. Providing services for participants with domestic abuse problems
H. Detecting and prosecuting fraus	
I. Providing transportation assistance	U. Providing services for participants with substance abuse problems
J. Ensuring continuing child care, MediCal and/or Food Stamps for families leaving aid	V. Promoting economic development
	W. Utilization of post employment/job retention services
K. Implementing sanctions	

6. Counties are using a variety of approaches to providing services to address special needs and barriers to work. Please indicate if you have a program to address the following needs and how you deliver the program. Check the box on the right if no services are available for a specific barrier/need.

		How are these services provided?				
	SPECIAL NEEDS/BARRIERS	Directly by CalWORKs Agency	Through Welfare Dept. Contract with Nonprofit Provider	Through Welfare Dept. Contract with For Profit Provider	Referral/ MOU with Agencies Funded to Provide Service	OR, Check Here If Service Not Provided
		(Check All That Apply on Each Line)				
a)	No high school diploma ..	❏	❏	❏	❏	❏
b)	Limited literacy skills	❏	❏	❏	❏	❏
c)	No work experience	❏	❏	❏	❏	❏
d)	Chronic health problem/disability	❏	❏	❏	❏	❏
e)	Language barrier...............	❏	❏	❏	❏	❏
f)	Legal problems (warrants, convictions).....	❏	❏	❏	❏	❏
g)	Remote location/lack of transportation	❏	❏	❏	❏	❏

7. Does your county conduct home visits.....

		In All Cases	Pilot Project or Subset of Cases	Never or Almost Never
		(Check One Box on Each Line)		
a)	for new applicants before eligibility determination?	❏	❏	❏
b)	before sanctions are applied?	❏	❏	❏
c)	after a sanction has been applied?...............................	❏	❏	❏
d)	in other circumstances? Please specify:	❏	❏	❏

_____

52

8. Successful implementation often depends on adequate capacity in the community to deliver a needed service and on adequate funding to support the demand for a service. For example, some have argued that certain types of child care (e.g., infant care) are in short supply even though funding for child care demand may be adequate. Please indicate whether your county is having and/or anticipates having a shortage of service capacity and/or funding for each of the following services.

		A. CAPACITY SHORTFALL			B. FUNDING SHORTFALL		
		None	Current	Anticipated	None	Current	Anticipated
		(Check One Box on Each Line)			*(Check One Box on Each Line)*		
a)	Infant child care	❏	❏	❏	❏	❏	❏
b)	After school child care	❏	❏	❏	❏	❏	❏
c)	Mildly ill child care	❏	❏	❏	❏	❏	❏
d)	Off hours/weekend child care	❏	❏	❏	❏	❏	❏
e)	Stage 1 child care	❏	❏	❏	❏	❏	❏
f)	Stage 2 child care	❏	❏	❏	❏	❏	❏
g)	Stage 3 child care	❏	❏	❏	❏	❏	❏
h)	GED/adult basic education classes	❏	❏	❏	❏	❏	❏
i)	ESL classes	❏	❏	❏	❏	❏	❏
j)	Alcohol and drug treatment	❏	❏	❏	❏	❏	❏
k)	Services for victims of domestic abuse	❏	❏	❏	❏	❏	❏
l)	Mental health services	❏	❏	❏	❏	❏	❏
m)	Foster care	❏	❏	❏	❏	❏	❏
n)	Vocational rehabilitation	❏	❏	❏	❏	❏	❏
o)	Job/vocational training	❏	❏	❏	❏	❏	❏
p)	Transportation services	❏	❏	❏	❏	❏	❏
q)	Community service jobs	❏	❏	❏	❏	❏	❏

9. Counties report difficulties in meeting the two-parent family participation rate. This question is about special barriers and issues that limit participation among two-parent families in your county. Please note any problems or challenges that are particularly prevalent or difficult for each group listed below.

Special Problems or Issues

(Select Codes From Below)

a) Two-parent <u>refugee</u> families   [ ] [ ] [ ]   Other, specify: _____
_____

b) Two-parent <u>immigrant</u> families   [ ] [ ] [ ]   Other, specify: _____
_____

c) Two-parent <u>non-refugee, non-immigrant</u> families   [ ] [ ] [ ]   Other, specify: _____
_____

PARTICIPATION BARRIERS AND ISSUES	
A. No high school diploma/GED	**I.** Language barriers: obtaining employment
B. Limited literacy skills	**J.** Language barriers: understanding and using CalWORKs
C. No work history/experience	
D. Mental health problems	**K.** Socio-cultural barriers
E. Substance abuse problems	**L.** Legal problems
F. Domestic abuse problems	**M.** Remote location
G. Chronic health problems/disability in family	**N.** Lack of transportation
H. Children ill or with special needs	

54

THIS PAGE INTENTIONALLY BLANK

10. Please indicate whether the CalWORKs rules listed below are presenting temporary or ongoing problems or are not a problem in your country <u>at this time</u>. Check the box on the far right if you anticipate a future problem.

CalWORKs RULES	Not A Problem At This Time	Startup/ Transitional Problem Only	Minor Ongoing Problem	Major Ongoing Problem	AND Check Here If You Anticipate A Future Problem
(Check One Box on Each Line)					
a) 18/24-month work requirement	❑	❑	❑	❑	❑
b) Work participation rates for one-parent assistance units	❑	❑	❑	❑	❑
c) Work participation rates for two-parent assistance units	❑	❑	❑	❑	❑
d) Child support cooperation	❑	❑	❑	❑	❑
e) School attendance for children in assistance units	❑	❑	❑	❑	❑
f) Immunization	❑	❑	❑	❑	❑
g) Coordination of three stages of child care	❑	❑	❑	❑	❑
h) Monitoring participation in approved work activities	❑	❑	❑	❑	❑
i) Due process before sanctioning	❑	❑	❑	❑	❑
j) Vendor voucher payment system	❑	❑	❑	❑	❑
k) Child care monthly report (CW115)	❑	❑	❑	❑	❑
l) Monitoring/reporting on county performance outcomes	❑	❑	❑	❑	❑
m) Self Initiated Plans (SIPs)	❑	❑	❑	❑	❑
n) Determining waivers for good cause	❑	❑	❑	❑	❑
o) Sanctions	❑	❑	❑	❑	❑
p) Coordination with Welfare to Work grant providers	❑	❑	❑	❑	❑
q) New income/grant structure rules	❑	❑	❑	❑	❑
r) New property rules	❑	❑	❑	❑	❑

CalWORKs RULES	Not A Problem At This Time	Startup/ Transitional Problem Only	Minor Ongoing Problem	Major Ongoing Problem	AND Check Here If You Anticipate A Future Problem
	(Check One Box on Each Line)				
s) New transfer of assets rules	❑	❑	❑	❑	❑
t) Implementation of new penalties	❑	❑	❑	❑	❑
u) Other, please specify	❑	❑	❑	❑	❑

_____

11. What is the period of exemption in your county for participants...

    a.   when they have a first child after beginning to participate in CalWORKs?   _____ Months

    b.   who have a second child while participating in CalWORKs?   _____ Months

12. Did your county extend the 18-month CalWORKs time limit for all new applicants to 24 months?

    ❑ Yes   ❑ No

13. Last year, counties could choose the number of hours that single parent cases were required to work or participate in approved welfare to work activities. How many hours were required to meet the participation requirement in your county as of July 1, 1998?

    _____ Hours per week

14. How is your county spending (planning to spend) its incentive funds? *(Check all that apply)*

    ❑ Not yet planned/allocated   ❑ New staff   ❑ New programs, specify:

    ❑ Capital improvements   ❑ Other, specify: _____

    ❑ Reserve   _____   _____

    _____   _____

15. During the past 12 months has the caseload increased, decreased or remained about the same for:

	Increased	Decreased	Remained About the Same	Don't Know
			(Check One)	
a) most eligibility caseworkers?	❑	❑	❑	❑
b) most employment/welfare to work caseworkers?	❑	❑	❑	❑

16. Characteristics of county welfare populations, economic environments, and existing government structures have sometimes been cited as hindering or facilitating CalWORKs implementation. Please indicate whether, in your opinion, each of the following has hindered, facilitated, or had no effect on implementation of CalWORKs in your county during the past year.

		Greatly Hindered	Slightly/ Somewhat Hindered	No Known Effect/Too Soon To Tell	Slightly/ Somewhat Facilitated	Greatly Facilitated
		(Check One Box on Each Line)				
a)	Supply of entry level jobs	❏	❏	❏	❏	❏
b)	Location of entry level jobs	❏	❏	❏	❏	❏
c)	Supply of "better" jobs	❏	❏	❏	❏	❏
d)	Seasonality of work	❏	❏	❏	❏	❏
e)	Local unemployment rate	❏	❏	❏	❏	❏
f)	Procuring additional office space	❏	❏	❏	❏	❏
g)	County limits on hiring	❏	❏	❏	❏	❏
h)	Supply of low income housing	❏	❏	❏	❏	❏
i)	Public transportation	❏	❏	❏	❏	❏
j)	Language/cultural barrier	❏	❏	❏	❏	❏
k)	Welfare agency culture	❏	❏	❏	❏	❏
l)	Size and budget of welfare agency	❏	❏	❏	❏	❏
m)	Availability of qualified staff for CalWORKs positions	❏	❏	❏	❏	❏
n)	Welfare agency staff experience	❏	❏	❏	❏	❏
o)	Welfare agency computer systems	❏	❏	❏	❏	❏
p)	Welfare agency staff training	❏	❏	❏	❏	❏
q)	Interagency relationships	❏	❏	❏	❏	❏
r)	Contracting for services	❏	❏	❏	❏	❏
s)	Other, please specify	❏	❏	❏	❏	❏

THIS PAGE INTENTIONALLY BLANK

17. Which CalWORKs managers receive regular (at least quarterly) statistical reports on the following categories of participants?

		County Level Senior Management	District Managers	Supervisors	OR, Check Here If No Statistical Reporting
		(Check One Box on Each Line)			
a)	Participants enrolled in welfare to work activities	❑	❑	❑	❑
b)	Participants employed	❑	❑	❑	❑
c)	Participants employed 32 hours	❑	❑	❑	❑
d)	Participants failing to attend Job Club	❑	❑	❑	❑
e)	Participants declared exempt	❑	❑	❑	❑
f)	Participants sanctioned	❑	❑	❑	❑
g)	Participants out of compliance with work activity participation requirements	❑	❑	❑	❑
h)	Diversions	❑	❑	❑	❑
i)	Participants approaching 18/24-month limit	❑	❑	❑	❑
j)	Participants approaching 60-month time limit	❑	❑	❑	❑
k)	Participants meeting TANF work requirements	❑	❑	❑	❑
l)	Participants enrolled in Welfare to Work grant program services	❑	❑	❑	❑
m)	Participants with SIPs	❑	❑	❑	❑
n)	Participants using subsidized child care	❑	❑	❑	❑
o)	Participants referred to mental health services	❑	❑	❑	❑
p)	Participants utilizing mental health services	❑	❑	❑	❑

60

	County Level Senior Management	District Managers	Supervisors	OR, Check Here If No Statistical Reporting
	(Check One Box on Each Line)			
q) Participants referred to substance abuse services	❏	❏	❏	❏
r) Participants utilizing substance abuse services	❏	❏	❏	❏
s) Participants referred to domestic violence services	❏	❏	❏	❏
t) Participants utilizing domestic violence services	❏	❏	❏	❏

18. If possible, please include one recent example of each of the reports available to county level senior management.

19. During the past 12 months, has your county increased the number of CalWORKs eligibility or welfare to work caseworkers by either hiring for new positions or filling existing vacancies? *(Check one)*

      ❏ Hired for new positions

      ❏ Filled vacancies

      ❏ Both

      ❏ Neither

      ❏ Don't know

20. During the past 12 months, has your county increased the number of supervisory and/or CalWORKs management staff either by hiring for new positions or filling existing vacancies? *(Check one)*

      ❏ Hired for new positions

      ❏ Filled vacancies

      ❏ Both

      ❏ Neither

      ❏ Don't know

21. Major organizational changes in local government have accompanied the adoption of welfare reform in some counties. To enable the evaluation to gauge these changes, please provide a copy of the current organizational chart for the agency or agencies charged with the overall administration of CalWORKs, including TANF and welfare to work programs. If major organizational changes are anticipated over the next 6 months, please include a copy, if available, of the proposed organization chart for the agency or agencies within which CalWORKs will be administered.

22. This questionnaire may not have addressed all the CalWORKs implementation issues of importance in your county. Please use this space or attach additional pages if you wish to add comments about your implementation experiences, problems, and successes.

_____

_____

_____

_____

_____

_____

_____

_____

_____

_____

_____

_____

_____

_____

_____

Thank you for taking the time to complete this questionnaire.

Further information on RAND's statewide CalWORKs evaluation is available online at http://www.rand.org/CalWORKs. The survey results will be available mid-February 2000.

References

Ebener, Patricia A., and Jacob Alex Klerman. *Welfare Reform in California: Results of the 1998 All-County Implementation Survey.* Santa Monica, Calif.: RAND, MR-1052-CDSS, 1999.

Klerman, Jacob, Tammi Chun, Patricia Ebener, Donna Farley, Nicole Humphrey, Elaine Reardon, and Gail Zellman. *Welfare Reform in California: State and County Implementation of CalWORKs in the Second Year.* Santa Monica, Calif.: RAND, MR-1177-CDSS, 2000.

Zellman, Gail, Jacob Klerman, Elaine Reardon, and Paul Steinberg. *Welfare Reform in California: State and County Implementation of CalWORKs in the Second Year, Executive Summary.* Santa Monica, Calif.: RAND, MR-1177/1-CDSS, 2000.